If you are looking to transform your relationships, your career and your life, this book will provide the foundation to achieving all of that. I found it utterly life-changing.

Mitch Harris, Founder, Pocket Blockbuster

This learning has changed the way I view the world for the better.

Amy Higham, Commercial Manager, M&S

This is radical, life-changing learning which has had phenomenal impact on me. I feel like I've been fast-tracked to success.

Kristian Trend, Group Manager, Sodexo

It has changed how I see myself, others and what is possible. I can't recommend it highly enough.

Sebastian Brixey-Williams, Co-director, BASIC (British American Security Information Council)

This learning has the opportunity to transform education – we need it at the heart of everything we teach in schools as well as at the heart of our organisations.

Jonny McCausland, Head Boy, Wellington College

If asked to say in one word how this learning has made me feel, I'd say 'unboxed'. Quite simply, it's showed me that the barriers which box us in are self-imposed and whilst there might be some measure of comfort in their familiarity, there's much more joy and impact without them.

Maryanna Nwosisi, Associate, Slaughter & May

I can't articulate well enough just how differently I look at life now. Everyone needs to learn this.

Hannah Smith, Business Partner, L'Oréal

This has taught me more about myself than I've learnt in my 27 years... I'm so thankful I've learnt this now, when I have enough chance to make a difference.

Katy Johnston, Transformation and Strategic Execution Lead, Aviva

This learning truly provides the tools to take ownership of your life – so if that is you, you need this book.

James Jefferson-Loveday, Head of Careers and Housemaster, Magdalen College School, Oxford

Elke's experience, expertise and, above all, her well-founded and wholehearted belief in this kind of human development make devoting time and effort to this rich source of learning, essential.

Ben Vessey, Headmaster, Canford School

This is different. It focuses on who you really are and how you actually become the person you want to be. I found it invaluable, both personally and professionally.

Anil Sarda, Partnerships Manager, *The Economist*

This forces you to go deep – really understand who you are and from that place create the life that is right for you. Perfect for people that are prepared to lead their lives.

Lina Kehlenbeck, Group Head of Technology, Sainsbury's and Argos

Elke's message is about values-driven, purposeful leadership that derives from self-knowledge and an ability to create relationships on trust. It's a highly inspiring, hopeful vision of what leadership can be, but it's more than that: it is a feet-on-the-ground perspective, rich with good sense and understanding, spoken with passion and authority by someone who knows her subject.

Jonnie Noakes,
Director of Teaching and Learning, Eton College

Brilliant in every way. Thank you for showing me how to live MY life and become the kind of leader people need and want.

Luke Kenny, Consultant, Accenture

I have read hundreds of books, and this one stopped me in my tracks. It is simply brilliant. Humble, honest, accessible, it is packed with pragmatic tools that are truly life-changing. We all need this learning – and the sooner the better.

Sean Spurgin, Director of Leadership and Learning, Blue Sky

Everyone needs access to this learning; it is profound and game-changing.

Stephen Kakouris, Business Analyst, Shell

This learning is unique and life-changing. I can't tell you how grateful I am for having found it – I have grown in confidence, and have real clarity around the skills that matter.

Ayobami Kuteyi, Senior Manager, Google

RETHINK PRESS

First published in Great Britain in 2020 by
Rethink Press (www.rethinkpress.com)

Contact the author:
Via LinkedIn: Elke Edwards
www.IvyHouse.co.uk

Cover design: Patrick Fogarty and Laura Jelly
Illustrations: Patrick Fogarty
Back cover image: Alun Callender

HOW TO LEAD
A
BIGGER,
BRAVER,
MORE
MEANINGFUL
LIFE

EXTRAORDINARY

ELKE EDWARDS

*For Maggie and Uwe, who gave me
the courage to find my own path.*

Contents

Tell me, who are you to think yourself so small?

The Reason Why

In January 2015, I stood in the boardroom of a global bank in London, staring out at the city below me. I was so far up it felt like I was looking down on a toy town. As I always did before a coaching session, I cleared my mind to ensure I was fully present for my client, then turned to smile as he walked in.

I had no idea that what was about to happen would change my life forever.

Richard's coaching session started as usual, with a litany of what was going wrong with his business. Forty-one years old and the high-flying head of a tax division, Richard had been working with me for five months, and every session was roughly the same. First, he got more and more frustrated as he listed all the ways in which pressure was being put on him by shareholders, the City and his team. Then he moved on to his personal life. He and his wife were ever more distant, and they had just learnt that their eldest daughter was self-harming. He felt helpless about what to do. It seemed like his wife was blaming him for the issues in their family, and this made him angry. In his mind, the children and house were her domain. What's more, his health was suffering, and he felt continually anxious about the state of the world. Obviously, he explained, he loved his wife and children. He wanted to make a positive impact on the planet, as well as make good money. But he just couldn't be responsible for everything.

We were 20 minutes into the session when Richard suddenly stopped talking.

"Are you okay?" he asked.

"Yes, why?" I responded.

"Elke," he said, "you're crying."

And I was. I had tears streaming down my face. They didn't seem to want to stop.

"I can't do this anymore," I finally managed to choke out. "It's too hard."

Richard looked a bit confused "But I was told you were one of the best coaches around," he said.

"I can't keep working with people who say they want things to change but aren't prepared to DO or THINK differently," I burst out. "People who aren't willing to be the leaders of their own lives. It is like pushing water up a hill."

He sat back in his chair, staring at me for a moment. "Okay," he said eventually. "Seeing as you seem to be dumping me, and, as this will probably be our last session, can I make a request?"

I nodded, unable to talk through my tears.

"Before you go, will you tell me what you mean by 'being the leaders of their own lives'? Isn't that exactly what I'm doing? I've been a straight-A student all my life, I went to a leading university, I'm at the top of the career ladder and I've worked with the top coaches. What is it I haven't learnt?" He stopped for a moment then quietly mumbled, without actually looking at me: "Why don't you actually tell me what you mean as opposed to just walking away?"

And then it struck me. I had let both of us down in a massive way.

I'd been working in the field of human potential for over 20 years and during this time I'd come to realise that the way we'd been helping people to "succeed" didn't work. Research was consistently showing that people in affluent parts of the world were richer and better educated, with more leisure time than previous generations, but it also showed that we were more anxious, depressed, stressed, and lonely than ever before.[12]

So, as I'd coached some of the country's top thought leaders, business leaders, writers, professional sports people and actors, I became fascinated by what *really* worked. With so many living case studies to draw from, I began to identify what exactly made the difference between someone who seemed to be doing fine (but wasn't really) and someone who was genuinely living a bigger, braver, more meaningful life.

The years went by: I founded and then sold an award-winning performance development business, gave talks around the world, and worked with senior leaders and teams from the likes of Virgin, Barclays, Centrica, Linklaters, NatWest, the BBC, EE, Aviva and Sky. I slowly began to understand that there was a certain set of skills that, when mastered, made a game-changing difference to how anyone's life turned out.

At the same time as I had begun to learn more about what 'success' really meant and how to get it, I had begun to realise that my life, like those of so many of my clients, also looked fine on the outside but didn't feel fine on the inside. I had two gorgeous girls and a successful career, I lived in a beautiful house with a charming, bright husband. We had a great group of friends and family, and lovely holidays. But in quiet moments I couldn't help but notice that, deep inside, I had a feeling of emptiness. A feeling that I wasn't truly connected to this seemingly wonderful life I was living.

So one day, in June 2008, I had finally admitted that my marriage, in fact the life I had created, wasn't what I wanted and it was time to be honest with myself. I left the family home with two young girls, moved into a rental property and decided it was time to find my one true life. The one I knew was waiting for me, if only I had the courage to find it. It was the hardest thing I have ever done. It caused a lot of pain for the people I loved most. But I genuinely knew that I had no choice.

Aside from my daughters, I was starting with a blank sheet of paper. It was exciting… and terrifying. As a lifelong self-development nut, I searched in vain to find THE book – the one that would help me finally find my extraordinary life. But none of them quite spoke to all my worries and needs; none of them went deep enough. As a result, I went on the most extreme, cobbled-together learning journey – taking course after course, studying book after book, working with coaches and teachers of all kinds.

What followed was the wholesale transformation of my life. I took time to learn who I really was and what I really wanted, changed my role to focus solely on coaching and leadership, moved houses and met and married a wonderful man – one who is completely different from who I 'thought' would be right for me. Together we've brought together two distinct families, involving five teenage girls, to create an unorthodox but extraordinary family.

So, on that day back in 2015, when Richard challenged me, I realised that I had never truly shared what I'd discovered. Working on instinct, I'd become good at helping my clients develop as individuals, but I'd never laid those transformative skills out in one place.

I also realised that I'd never been totally honest with him. Because those skills only worked for people who were prepared to own their own lives, people who accepted that the quality of their life was down to them and were prepared to learn and do what it took to get the lives they wanted. Before we'd started to work together, I should have checked in with Richard – was that him? Because, if not, I wouldn't be able to help.

When Richard said he "just couldn't be responsible for everything", it was a huge red flag. In that moment I think I'd realised it wasn't going to work. Though we can't be responsible for other people or events beyond our control, we do need to take responsibility for our own lives. Whatever certain self-help gurus may say, we can't control the vast, wild, unknowable universe with 'positive thinking' or 'an abundance mindset'. Life is always going to be full of obstacles and pain as well as opportunity and joy. But we can always take full responsibility for how we experience what happens around us. Always.

If, right at the start of our first ever session, I had checked in on whether or not Richard was truly ready to be the leader of his own life – whether he was prepared to get to know himself deeply and take action based on what he learned – we might not have wasted five months of our lives on ineffectual coaching. Thankfully my meltdown led to a breakthrough for us both.

It also led, a year later, to a new business and now, to this book – *Extraordinary*.

Extraordinary is for people who want to be the leaders of their lives. It's for people who don't want to leave their life to chance and are not going to spend the next five, ten or thirty years feeling that they have no say in their level of happiness. It's for people who are fed up with the status quo and are determined to be the change in the world around them.

In some ways it is a leadership book, in that it is the perfect foundation for people who want to become leaders, whether of a business, a community or a family. But it is also far more than that – it is a rallying call for every single person out there who knows deep inside them there is an extraordinary life waiting for them, a bigger, braver and more meaningful life.

If that is you, I am glad we've found each other.

Let's Talk Extraordinary

"The truth will set you free, but it will piss you off first."
Gloria Steinem

What if life wasn't difficult? What if life was just life, and what made it good or bad was completely down to you? What if confidence, joy, wellbeing and inner peace were already inside you – sitting there twiddling their thumbs until the moment you needed them – and you could access them whenever you wanted?

You can. Not because I say you can, but because it is true. Like the earth is round and gravity can't be denied, this is a fact of life. You may think that you were born broken, that other people have a greater talent for happiness than you, or that you need to learn some mysterious 'secret' of success. The self-help industry makes $10 billion globally[3] from persuading you that's the case, and it couldn't be more wrong. Confidence, wellbeing, inner peace, joy, these are available to us all – all of the time. The huge problem is that somehow, in this dysfunctional world we have created, we have forgotten how to find them.

The purpose of this book is to show you how to do just that. During my career working with all these incredible people I realised that there are seven skills, seven transformational skills, that make an extraordinary difference to how people's lives turn out. The purpose of this book is to share these skills with you.

I warn you now: my advice won't be for everyone. This book is only for a certain type of person: those who are prepared to take charge of their lives. It's for people who want to be leaders: thought leaders, activists, artists breaking new ground, CEOs, politicians, researchers, community leaders, educational leaders... and also those who simply want to have a positive impact on those around them in their schools, organisations and homes. It is for those that believe there is a better way than the one laid out before them. And it is for people willing to do what it takes to get them there.

It is not a promise of pain-free living, however. Quite the opposite. As you build your extraordinary life you will experience the whole gamut of emotions - joy, fear, anger, frustration and everything in between – just as human beings were designed to do. The difference is you won't let them overwhelm you – you will relish the joy and excitement as it passes through you and feel the sadness and fear as they come and go. You will befriend your feelings, use them productively, without getting stuck in spirals and feel the deep joy of living your 'right' life.

And, if you're looking for a fool-proof plan to climb the career ladder, look elsewhere. That's one of the reasons we've got into this mess; too many people climb that ladder only to realise they don't like the view from the top. It will, however, show you how to find work you love, so that you can truly engage and thrive at what you do – whether that's as a lawyer or a circus acrobat.

Finally, I am sorry to say, it won't help you find the love of your life... but it will show you, when you've found them, how to create a relationship based on authenticity and trust. A relationship that can get through the inevitable tough times because you know how to have proper conversations, be transparent and cope with having different views. Extraordinary ever after, you might say.

Here's how it works. Each chapter covers one skill. Each one, when mastered, will make a game-changing difference to your life. Put them all together and the impact is transformational. I'll share these skills with you by telling stories – every one of which is true. Stories that include a 17-year-old trying to carve a different future for himself, a CEO looking for meaning, a rock star with massive anxiety, and a twenty-something struggling with judging his divorced parents. These are stories of real people I've supported in their mission to become extraordinary, whether they're top business leaders I've come across in my coaching practice or the emerging leaders and teenagers I've met through the programmes we run at Ivy House. Irrespective of your age, sex, or situation, there is learning in each story for you. The CEO can learn from the teenager just as much as the teenager can learn from the CEO.

Yes, I founded Ivy House with the aim to empower the next generation to build better lives, and a better collective future, but you can become part of this movement at any age. You can change the direction of your life halfway through your career, just as well as you can if you're starting out. We need as many rebels as we can get.

I will ask you a lot of questions. Many of them will ask you to reach very deep into your own feelings, fears, hopes and beliefs. I know how tough that can be. I found it incredibly hard myself the first time I tried. And although it is important to answer these questions, it's even more important to understand the change you want to create, to get excited, and to fully commit. So I suggest you start by reading the whole book once through, as fast as you can, skipping over the questions. Then, once you've digested what it really means to live an extraordinary life, and decided to go for it, you can grab a notebook and truly get to work.

Because, remember, nothing is going to change until you do that work – and keep doing it. As your extraordinary life unfolds, as you grow and develop, and as life throws all its wonderful, terrible surprises your way, you'll want to return again and again to these questions and exercises to ensure that you are still heading exactly where you want to go.

So, I don't care if you are 15 or 55; he, she or they; at the peak of your career or trying to figure out which route to take. This book is for you if you want an extraordinary life and are prepared to take ownership for making it happen. A life with ups and downs, twists and turns, but one that is anchored in a feeling of wellbeing, confidence and joy that never leaves you. A life that has direction and purpose, is filled with people you love and people who love you. A life that adds to the world rather than taking from it.

It's crunch time. Don't waste a second more on reading if this doesn't set your heart on fire.

Make the decision now: are you in?

Core Strength

"Don't try and steer the river."
Deepak Chopra

A few months ago, I had a jam-packed day: a meeting with the CEO of a very successful tech start-up in the morning, and a talk at an inner-city school in the afternoon. Although I rarely take on new coaching assignments with senior leaders anymore, an old client had asked me to meet with Sanjay, who was really struggling. She described him as one of the brightest, hardest-working and most committed CEOs she had ever worked with, but it was clear that recently, something wasn't right.

When I walked in, he was the picture of success. Sharply dressed and evidently fit, he welcomed me into a stunning glass-walled office full of photos of his beautiful family, juxtaposed with original pieces of art. He was warm, calm and looked as if he had everything anyone could ever want. Sanjay, however, was deeply unhappy. Although on the outside his life looked picture-perfect, the reality was very different. But his story wasn't the usual checklist of CEO woes: work troubles, health issues, feeling disconnected from his family.

On the contrary, he was still deeply in love with his wife and seemed truly connected to his two sons. He was clearly very good at his job, with a flourishing team and happy investors.

No, his challenge was the feeling of emptiness he woke up with every morning and was unable to shake throughout the day. What had dawned on him – but he had never had the courage to admit – was that while he was very successful and adored his family, the life he was living was not 'his life'.

More and more, on a daily basis, Sanjay found himself daydreaming of being a photographer: travelling the world, living in different places and meeting people from all walks of life. He had never had any interest in the fancy restaurants and clubs he now frequented, but instead craved to sit in a beach café or a street market, trying the local food, experiencing the sights, smells and sounds. Yes, he wanted to be with his wife and sons, but he wanted them all to live a different life.

We did some deep work together that morning, and Sanjay's story was still lingering in my mind when I headed to the school in the afternoon. After I had given my talk, I was approached by a 17-year-old about to do his A-levels called Nick. Nick came from a close-knit family that had lived and worked in the same area for decades and was the first of them to stay in school past the age of 16. Most of his relatives worked as market traders, with his parents running a very successful fruit and veg business. When Nick had first mentioned he wanted to stay on in school, his mum had been really proud, telling everyone she knew that Nick was the bright one. His dad, on the other hand, didn't see the point. Nick was going to end up on the markets anyway, so why wait? He could be earning money now – having a laugh with his mates and paying a bit of rent for his room. His dad had even said, in a year or so, he would fund him to get his own stall – so really, what was the point of A-levels? He could learn everything he needed from his mum and dad.

Nick asked me what to do. He loved his parents and his brother, he loved his community, he loved knowing everyone and feeling part of something. But he also loved maths. He loved it so much he wanted to go to university and maybe even become a lecturer. However, he knew what his parents would say, he knew what the lads down the pub would say, and none of it was good. His dilemma was keeping him awake at night.

Core Strength – what is it?

Our Core Strength is what makes up who we are. It's like our personal blueprint. At its heart is our vision for our life (the one that we want to live, not the one others want us to live or the one society tells us we should want). It also includes our values, beliefs and our driving forces, the skills and talents that put us in our element, and eventually perhaps our purpose in life.

When we know who we are at our core, and we live from that place, we find our true strength – our personal power. It is the skill of finding and living your one authentic life; the life you were meant to live; the life that really works for you.

Why is Core Strength so important?

When we know who we are and we find our true life, everything becomes so much easier. Really. When we have a clear vision, know which direction to head in and understand our personal values, making decisions becomes easy. When we are doing the right job or studying subjects that interest us, we learn quicker, we put in extra effort, and success is much easier to achieve. Living in this way is living from a position of strength. It allows you to become the person you were born to be and live the life you were born to live.

Let's go back to Sanjay for a moment. When Sanjay chose his career path and created his life, he did it with only a tiny percentage of the data available to him. He knew hardly anything about himself and, even more importantly, he didn't even know where or how to look. Without his personal blueprint, his life was like a house cobbled together with ill-fitting bricks, rather than a comfortable, vibrant home where he truly felt he belonged.

When Sanjay made his decision, here's what he thought he knew – and what he either didn't know or had forgotten.

What he thought he knew:
- He was bright and could do well at most things academically.
- He had a particular talent for coding.
- The school he went to thought he had made a wise choice when choosing a computer science degree.
- Artificial intelligence was a growth market and, if he was successful, he could make lots of money.
- Making lots of money would buy him the things that successful people had – including the things that would give his family a 'good' life.
- His parents would be proud of him if he followed this path.
- More than that, they would be pleased because it was the path that they had picked out.
- He had a belief that he would be letting his parents down if he didn't follow a path they would be proud of.

What he didn't know or had forgotten:

- His vision for his life included lots of 'off the beaten track' travel, meeting people from all walks of life.

- He was in his element when telling stories of people from many different cultures – he had always been happiest on holiday taking photographs.

- The happiest he had ever been was on a summer photography course he had been on.

- And the proudest he had ever felt was when two of his photographs had been printed in National Geographic.

- Being truly creative was the thing that brought him the most joy.

- He really didn't like living in cities.

- He had values around adventure, family, beauty and freedom.

- He didn't really crave a big house, fancy restaurants or designer clothes.

- The people he admired were filmmakers and photographers.

- He got bored of seeing the same people all the time.

- He had been brought up in a culture that valued financial success seemingly above all else.

- At school he was surrounded by friends that were choosing from a range of 'traditional', 'safe' careers that did not include the arts.

- He had never spent any time thinking about what success really meant for him.

The feeling of emptiness he was waking up with every day was nothing to do with the job he had chosen and everything to do with the job not being the right job for him. It was nothing to do with his Soho apartment not being lovely, but everything to do with this not being how he wanted to live.

Because here's the thing… we are all unique. And understanding that uniqueness is essential if you want an extraordinary life. Your brand of extraordinary is going to be different from mine. Which means taking time to figure out exactly what extraordinary means for you.

PAUSE AND REFLECT

What does success mean for you?

First, jot down any instinctive thoughts that come out of the question above, then answer the rest below. But remember, if this is your first time reading the book, it's perfectly okay to skip them. Just promise you'll come back.

- How do you want to feel inside?
- What kind of relationships do you want?
- What kind of people would you like to spend time with?
- What kind of things do you want to learn about?
- What experiences would you like to have?
- What would you like to achieve through your work?
- What things would you like to own?
- What would you like to be known for?
- What would you like to leave behind you when you go?

Life is a balancing act...

The figure below is demonstrating a yoga pose – the tree. Stand up for a moment and give it a go.

How did you do? How still were you? How strong did you feel? What did you do when you wobbled?

Chances are, if you have a really strong core, you were able to hold yourself pretty still. If something sent you off balance, you leant to one side, wobbled slightly and then – through your Core Strength – were able to right yourself. If your core isn't so strong, however, you probably found it much harder to balance.

All of life is like a tree pose. A lot of the time things seem fine and then all of a sudden something comes along out of the blue with the power to send us off balance.

If we are strong at our core, we are able to see the wobble for what it is and right ourselves pretty quickly. If we aren't, we will likely fall over, feel defeated, and maybe make a whole lot of drama getting back into balance. A successful life is not one without any wobbles; it is one in which we are able to handle what comes our way and quickly get back into alignment.

In yoga, your Core Strength is made up of the muscles that surround the abdomen, back and pelvis. In life, your Core Strength is made up of a different set of muscles: your vision, your purpose, your element, your beliefs, your values and your priority driving force. These are the things that make up the uniqueness of you, and only when you know them will you be able to stay aligned to the life you want to create.

What Nick learnt

Remember Nick, the 17-year-old I met at the school talk? As Nick and I started to chat I asked him some questions about his dream life. I asked him to imagine, if there were no constraints at all, where did he see himself living? With whom? What would he be doing for work? How would he feel inside? As he answered, it became obvious that he had a far clearer vision of his ideal life than he had realised. He told me about his dream house in Manchester, the kind of marriage he saw himself in, the three children he wanted, the cycling he would do at weekends and the book he was already planning to write.

Nick was fairly far down the road of having a clear vision – the first part of Core Strength. As we talked further, it also became obvious that he already had strong personal values around learning: giving back, safety, family and community. What he wasn't aware of, however, was that some of the beliefs he had were holding him back. Beliefs such as: 'People like me don't have lives like that,' 'I would never be a proper part of my family again,' 'I could never afford university,' 'I wouldn't have any mates there anyway because it's full of posh kids' – and so on.

Like so many of us, Nick needed to spend some time really getting to know himself, understanding the sort of life he wanted and the person he wanted to be. Until this point, he'd never realised that was even a thing. But once he did, I have never seen anyone attack the task with so much determination.

So how do you find all this stuff out about yourself?

When we teach Core Strength on our programmes at Ivy House, it takes people about two minutes to grasp the importance of it. Everyone completely gets that a life misaligned to their Core Strength would be a second-rate life. They realise – often for the first time – that living from Core Strength is about so much more than finding a career. Indeed, so many of us are so focused on finding the right job that we forget to find the right life. They also realise that they're seeing this mistake play out every day with the people around them – parents, relatives, friends and siblings.

So, the question that follows quickly is, how do I find out? How do I uncover all these secrets about myself so I can get on and build the perfect life?

BUT before we go down that route, we need to get a couple of things straight.

- Perfect is a dangerous word. It brings up visions of a life with no challenges, frustrations, problems or worries. We much prefer the term 'perfectly imperfect', which recognises that you can live a big, brave, meaningful life while dealing with a whole range of challenges that come your way. The Scottish philosopher and writer Syd Banks often said, "life is a contact sport," and I couldn't agree more. The aim isn't to avoid contact. It's to make as much contact as possible, yet still keep your balance.

- Finding your vision, purpose, element, beliefs, values and driving forces can take some time. After all, this is big stuff. Some will find answers pretty easily, like Nick, who already had an idea of what 'good' looked like for him. But others will really struggle. If that's you, please don't give up, panic, or judge yourself because you don't immediately know the answers. We've been trained for years in an education system that rewards knowing the answers, so it's natural to feel uncomfortable and frustrated when you don't. Just asking the questions puts you ahead of 99% of the population. Instead of feeling pressured to 'find your thing', be damn grateful that you now know Core Strength exists and you are about to go on an amazing journey to discover what makes up yours. And, accept that the journey may take time.

- Which doesn't, by the way, mean you should sit around navel-gazing until the answers magically drop into your lap. I've tried that strategy plenty of times and I have to tell you: IT DOESN'T WORK. Finding the answers requires you to a) ask yourself the questions, b) try out a whole load of stuff and c) stay alert to internal signs around what resonates. Effectively this means becoming an observer of your life, which is a reflective activity but by no means a passive one. After all, you will never discover your passion for abstract impressionism unless you go and see some. So, ask, experiment, notice – and repeat again and again. Try writing stuff down – keeping a 'thoughts journal' and see how your self-knowledge slowly builds.

- Even when you think you have nailed your answers, be aware that they will change. As you grow and evolve, so will your Core Strength. Your vision, your values and even your purpose could shift as time goes by and the universe flings curveballs your way. So, stay curious, and keep asking, experimenting and noticing. Come back to the questions in this section every few months and see if anything has changed. This is a journey of discovery that you are going to be on for the rest of your life. There is no big reveal, no cinematic climax; just the ever-evolving experience of what it means to be you. You'd better learn to enjoy the ride.

"Seriously, knowing my Core Strength has changed my life. For years I did things, some of which I enjoyed, but most of which I didn't. I always felt that other people knew something I didn't. Something which helped them find their 'right' life. It was like I had missed a crucial lesson in school and hadn't been given the work to catch up on.

Going through all the elements of Core Strength has been like someone cleaning my glasses. I finally see that I have been living as if by rote – following the same path as everyone else and hoping somehow that I would land in the right place. But guess what? I didn't. My job was boring, my relationship uninspiring and my life just felt grey. What I see now is that I was completely letting life happen to me. I wasn't taking ownership for actually figuring it out, let alone doing anything about it. But, now I've taken time to explore my Core Strength, I feel like I have finally woken up. I don't have it all clear in my head yet BUT I am so much clearer than I was. I realise that I have always had a limiting belief about what I am capable of and thought that my dream to work in software development was just that – a dream. I have realised that I really want to live abroad for a while… and that people like me can actually do that. And, having talked to my girlfriend, we have both realised that we want so much more in our relationship and are working on it together. We are like a different couple. So, I am good. I am really good. I feel strong. I know it isn't all going to fall out of the sky for me but at least I know what I want – honestly, I feel like a new man."

Shaun, 27 – (recently) in software development

Unearthing your Core Strength

What I am about to do now is something I really don't want to do. I am going to give you a list of things you need to find out about yourself. The reason I don't want to do this is because it's all too easy to activate the 'get the homework done/tackle the to-do list' gene, honed from years of school, university and work, and push on through the questions quickly in order to get the gold star.

Please, please, don't do that. That approach is a symptom of the broken system you're trying to escape. It will only take you further and further away from being in a place where you can be the observer, explorer and creator of your life. So, take your time. Get curious. Daydream. Ask people who you trust what they think. Make notes. Cross them out. Make some more. Expect the answers to change as you get to know yourself better. And remember: if this is your first time reading this book, feel free to leave the questions for later. Just make a commitment, now, that you'll come back to them.

The key elements of your Core Strength

1. Vision

In a minute, I want you to close your eyes and imagine yourself five or ten years in the future. You're going to watch yourself as if you're watching a movie. Where are you living? Who are you living with? Are you studying or working, neither or both? If you're studying, what are you studying? If you're working, what are you doing? If neither, what are you focused on? How do you spend your time? How much time do you spend on each element of your life? What are you excited about? What have you experienced? What are you looking forward to in your future?

Close your eyes and see the film play out. Try to engage all your senses. What do you see? What do you hear? What do you smell? And, importantly, how does it feel? Emotions are key here, as they are neurologically very much connected with long-term memory. Summon the feelings you want to experience, and your vision of the future will lodge itself that much more powerfully in your head.

Assuming you just played your movie, how was it? Are you excited? Did you see it in super-vivid ultra HD? Or was it a fuzzy, no-signal mess? Either is fine, because either way, what you just did was begin to create a vision for your life. We all need a vision – even if it changes a hundred times, even if you really struggle to figure it out. Visions guide us when we have important decisions to make, they inspire and motivate us through difficult times and, without them, it becomes very difficult to know which direction we should be heading in.

A vision is not just a picture of what life could be; it is an appeal to our better selves, a call to become something more. And that something more is what leads to an extraordinary life.

An effective vision covers every aspect of your life: your relation-ships, family, work, money, health, hobbies, who you want to be and how you want to feel. It is SO much more than a list of material goods you want to own, achievements or goals you want to reach. It is an inspiration, an image you can hold so close that you are motivated every day to move closer towards it. I like to think of the process of finding your vision as 'creating memories of the future' – memories it is now your job to bring to life.

Again, take some proper time to create it. To help, you can download our free exercise at IvyHouse.co.uk/Extraordinary. It will take you through the process to discover your life vision. Then, come back a week or so later and make any changes you want to make. Remember, this is an ongoing project – you should review your vision regularly and, as your understanding of yourself deepens, or as the life you want changes, you can keep adapting it to make sure that it really, truly sets your heart and soul alight.

2. Driving forces

Jody and Sara had been going out for five years when I met them on one of our first programmes. They had met in the first term of university and been together ever since. They clearly loved each other, but recently they had been arguing a lot, and they didn't really understand why. As we talked, it became clear that they both had different priorities. Sara was keen to settle down; she wanted to buy a house in the village she had grown up in and start a family. She wanted to feel safe, to know what was coming in the future and to have no surprises. Jody, on the other hand, was champing at the bit for adventure. She was ready to leave her job, go travelling and experience new things, and the last thing she wanted was a mortgage and a baby. It quickly became obvious that what was going on was a clash of driving forces. Every time the two of them talked, under the surface an epic battle between Certainty and Variety was playing out.

Look under the hood of any living human being, and you'll find driving forces motivating us. Jody and Sara learnt the hard way that these forces sit behind everything we do, whether or not we realise what's going on. Over the years, various thinkers have come up with descriptions of these forces; Maslow's Hierarchy of Needs and Anthony Robbins' Human Needs are two of the best known. At Ivy House, we focus in on the five driving forces that motivate all people at different times and to a different degree. They are: Certainty, Variety, Belonging, Recognition and Service.

Here are some examples of how the driving forces might play out. We may get a job so that we have Certainty around having food to eat and a roof over our heads. We try different things at the weekend to get Variety in our lives. We build families and friendships for Belonging, we strive to get better to achieve Recognition, and we do acts of Service for our communities so that we can feel part of something bigger than ourselves.

The first four driving forces are foundation forces – we literally need them to be met if we are going to function in a healthy way. The fifth force, Service, only comes into play once the other four are met. When we feel safe, loved, stimulated and recognised enough, we turn our minds to giving back. At this point, Service will often become a person's priority driving force – and they will get closer to extraordinary than ever before.

There are three important things you need to know about driving forces:

1. They are invisible to almost all of the population.
2. While we need all four of the foundation forces to be met all of the time, there is usually one that is your priority at any given moment.
3. And finally, they can be met in a negative or positive way – when we choose to meet the needs of our driving forces positively, we will be setting ourselves up for success. If, however, we fall into getting them met negatively, we will be contributing to our own downfall.

What happened with Sara and Jody isn't unusual – they simply started to want different things as they grew. Their priority driving forces had shifted since they first met, but because they didn't understand what was happening, they got caught in a cycle of blame and upset. Sara blamed Jody for taking her away from her family and not committing. Jody blamed Sara for being boring and never wanting to go out or try new things. When they finally understood what was going on between them, they were both able to calm down and have an honest conversation about what they each wanted. For them, that meant deciding to lovingly end their relationship, be free to create the lives they wanted and continue as friends.

Having different priority driving forces doesn't necessarily mean the end of a relationship. But you do have to find a way to get both of your needs met in a positive, rather than a negative, way.

Cassie seemed to have it all: a loving family, good grades and a large group of friends. She also had a priority driving force of Recognition. Without knowing it, Cassie had learnt to get this need met by being a 'drama queen'. She made sure she always had some crisis or other going on in order to get attention, so her friends would gather around her and try everything they could to help. Cassie also got her need for Recognition met by bitching about one group of friends with another. This not only made her feel important, it also met her secondary need of Belonging.

Clearly, Cassie had a choice – although I'm pretty sure she didn't know it at the time. Like all of us, Cassie wanted to meet the needs of her driving forces, but she had, probably unconsciously, chosen to do it in a negative way. She could have got her need for Recognition met by being a truly great friend who was fun to be around. She could have got it met by becoming good at something or going out of her way to support someone in need. All of these would be positive ways of satisfying her priority driving force – if only she'd known. Instead she got a reputation for being a drama queen and a bitch. Eventually her friends, finding her untrustworthy and draining to be around, began to avoid her. Her choices backfired.

> "When I learnt about the Driving Forces, I realised that I was meeting my need for Recognition in a really negative way. I am the Finance Director of a huge business and work very closely with my senior team – trust is really important, and I talk about it with them all the time. At the same time, though, I realise I spend a lot of time talking badly about certain members of my team with my PA and my Business Manager. It is like I want them to see me as a martyr for what I have to put up with. I realise now, I wanted them to see how much pressure I am under, so they feel sorry for me and would give me attention in this way. I do it with my

husband too: I am always telling him how tough my job is so he can keep telling me how good I am. I have got to say it is really hard to admit this – really hard – and I hated it when the coach called me on it. But I realise now I have been doing it all my life and I want it to change. I don't want to be that person. I know people like that – the people that are always seeking attention by playing the victim, and I really don't like them. Basically, I have to find a way of getting my need for Recognition met positively. I know now it is okay to want and need recognition – we all do. But there are ways of getting it that don't make you a disloyal and unkind person and that is what I need to learn."

Sara, 51, finance director of a commercial airline

PAUSE AND REFLECT

What's driving you?

What do you think your priority driving force is right now?

How are you getting it met positively?

How are you getting it met negatively?

What do you want to do about that?

3. Values

There is a lot of talk in society about personal values. But what is a personal value? A value is something that is very, very important to you. Important to the extent that if it is not in your life, it will actually impact on your wellbeing. For example, if you have a personal value around freedom and you are in a relationship where your partner monitors your every move, you will start to feel constrained, frustrated and may even become unwell. Conversely, if you are in a relationship with a partner that respects your value of freedom you will feel energised, strong and begin to thrive.

For a very short period, I worked for a boss who didn't want any kind of relationship with me outside a functional one. I would ask him how he was each morning; he would say "fine"and walk straight into his office. In meetings, I would sometimes share what was going on in my life or what I had done at the weekend. He showed no interest and shared nothing about himself. After a few months, even though I loved the work I was doing, I woke up and knew I had to leave. I just couldn't go on working for a boss that I had no relationship with. For others, it may have felt like freedom; for me, it felt empty and wrong. What I didn't know then was that one of my core values was connection.

Knowing your individual values means understanding yourself at the deepest level. It means you can make decisions based on what really matters to you, and help partners, bosses and friends truly understand where you're coming from. It means that you can quickly understand why you might be feeling out of balance and know what to do to get back into your tree pose! The problem is, you would be blown away by how many people have no idea what their values are, and spend years living out of alignment because of it. You may even know one or two.

I would love to tell you that all it takes to discover your values is a quick exercise. In reality, in my experience, it is a longer and deeper journey than that.The good news is that you can start that exploratory work now by asking yourself the five key values questions:

1. What needs to be in your life for it to be fulfilling for you?
2. What needs to be in your relationships for them to work for you?
3. What frustrates you in others? (You probably value the thing they don't do.)
4. What do you really appreciate/respect in others?
5. What makes you joyful?

These are not 'one sitting' questions. Get a notebook and brainstorm them, then set the notebook aside. Over the next few weeks mull over the questions, even put them on sticky notes around your house, and jot down anything else that comes to mind. Here are just some examples of values that might help, although this is by no means an exhaustive list.

Authenticity	Achievement	Adventure	Balance
Beauty	Boldness	Challenge	Compassion
Contribution	Creativity	Curiosity	Determination
Fairness	Friendships	Fun	Growth
Happiness	Honesty	Humour	Influence
Kindness	Learning	Love	Loyalty
Openness	Optimism	Popularity	Recognition
Security	Spirituality	Stability	Status
Success	Trustworthiness	Wealth	

Next, give the 'values questions' above to people that know you and ask them to answer them on your behalf.

What would they say needs to be in your life, frustrates you, makes you joyful? Ask as many people as you can and add their data to your own. Over time you will notice some things start repeating themselves and you will find you are getting closer and closer to understanding your core values.

If this is your first time reading this book, just keep reading. But perhaps, when you come back to tackle the questions, your brain will have already come up with a few ideas. Brains work like that.

When you have clarity about your values, so many other things will become clear to you. Why you like some people and not others. Why some things make you angry and others don't. More importantly, you will be able to make decisions that are aligned to your values. For example, if you have a value around wealth, it will rule out a number of jobs for you. If you have a value around community, it will influence where you live. If you have a value around environment, it will influence what you eat and how you travel. Put all three together – wealth, community and environment – and again, it will mean different choices. Remember there are no right or wrong values – only ones that matter to you so much you can't live without them, and the ones that don't.

4. Beliefs

"I work and live with my boyfriend. On one particular day, I'd been unwell and left the office promptly at 5.30 to have a bath and curl up. He said he would just finish up and be right behind me. I got home, ran a bath, cooked dinner for us both and waited. And waited. I rang his mobile, but it went straight to voicemail, so I just kept sending messages and waiting... for five hours. By the time he got home, having apparently been out with his best mate all night, I was fuming... I told him that, if he loved me, he would have come straight home and made sure I was okay. If he respected me, he would've at least texted and told me about his changing plans. And, because I had no idea that they were just my beliefs, I wholeheartedly believed I was right. My boyfriend, on the other hand, had a different set of beliefs. He believed that you should live for the moment and, when his mate suggested a drink on a lovely sunny evening, he believed the right thing to do was to grasp the moment. He had texted me (it hadn't arrived) and then decided to turn off his phone, so he could be fully present for his mate. He believed that because I was ill, I would want peace and quiet and he wanted to give me that. He said this didn't mean that he didn't love me and couldn't understand why I would think it would."

Paula, 31, social media manager

Beliefs aren't right or wrong; they're just thoughts that we buy into. The problem is that most of us buy into them to such an extent that we believe them to be unshakeably true. You may hold the belief, for example, that people who live in big houses, drive fast cars and have high-profile jobs are successful. Your belief may extend to the point that you believe that people who have these things are better than people who do not. But these are just thoughts that you have bought into. They are not truth. There is a BIG difference.

We all have a set of beliefs that we deem to be true. For example, you might believe that going to a good university will make the difference between success and failure in your life. Or you might believe that going to university will create a whole load of debt, and mean you miss out on three years' work experience that will make you far more valuable to an employer. Both valid. Neither true.

The beliefs we carry around with us are our lens on the world. They are like those glasses you have to put on for an eye test – the ones that can carry lots of lenses at once and give you a very distorted view of whatever you're looking at.

The problem with our 'belief glasses' is that we don't know we are wearing them. We think we are seeing the world exactly as it is, when what we are really seeing is just our view of it, based on a random set of collected beliefs. Beliefs we collected from a whole load of random places – our family, school, community, the culture we grew up in. Like our accent, they were handed down to us, without us even knowing. When we were children, we had an operating system installed inside us, without being told about it and without any say on how it ran. Until now.

To demonstrate just how random our belief systems are, think about something you believe in strongly – it could be about politics, diversity, climate change or the perfect length of fake eyelashes. Then imagine someone born on exactly the same day as you but in a different country, to a family with completely different financial circumstances, political affiliations and religious persuasions. Do you think they would believe what you believe? I doubt it. And, which one of you is right? Neither of you are. All you are doing is holding on to a set of thoughts that, because of your upbringing, you believe to be true.

The challenge for us all then is to be aware of our beliefs. To be aware if they are serving us or hindering us, aware if they are tricking us into thinking we are right and everyone else is wrong. And make a conscious decision about WHETHER we want to continue seeing life through the random set of beliefs we have collected along the way OR, if we want to build our own lens.

There are two types of beliefs you need to become aware of:

1. Empowering Beliefs

Empowering beliefs serve us, they help us achieve the life of our dreams. They sound like this:

- I am strong and resilient and always achieve my goals.
- I am confident and funny and get on well with others.
- I am blessed with amazing family and friends.

2. Limiting Beliefs

Limiting beliefs, however, hold us back, stop us doing things and often make us feel awful as well. They sound like this:

- I am not as clever as my mates and will never do as well.
- People like me don't get jobs like that.
- I am ugly and fat and no one will ever fancy me.

When we carry limiting beliefs around with us and see them as facts, they impact how we behave and, as a result, impact the outcomes we get in life. But here's the brilliant thing. We don't have to carry any beliefs around that don't serve us. In the same way we picked them up, we can also put them down. You can decide not to take that belief with you going forward and replace it with one that strengthens you instead.

For example:

This...

- I am not as clever as my mates and will never do as well.
- People like me don't get jobs like that.
- I am ugly and fat and no one will ever fancy me.

Becomes this...

- I can do brilliantly in a career that I care about.
- If I am passionate and work hard then there is no reason for me not to get the job.
- There is someone for everyone and I am going to enjoy finding the person who loves me for me.

The even better news is that your brain supports you to do just that.

> "I have spent my whole life believing I was shy. All of it. Like, I totally believed some people were just born that way. When I was told that wasn't the case, I was angry. I felt like I was being judged, and that they didn't understand that I just didn't have any choice – that I really was just born shy and it was nothing to do with me. And then, one day, in drama, I had to play a really cocky gangster, and, in that moment, I got it. When I was playing the gangster, I believed I was a king, like I was the most powerful person around, that could do anything I wanted, and I did. I strutted across that stage like I owned it. The next day I remembered this moment as I walked into school – without me really trying too hard I just started to walk a bit differently, with a bit more confidence and God, I felt different."
>
> Robbie, 17, A-level student

How to clean your glasses

To understand how to let your limiting beliefs go and replace them with ones that empower you, we are going to have to dig into a bit of neuroscience. Our brains are made up of a whole load of neural pathways which, when put together, effectively make up our personal operating system. The primary cells in our brains are called neurons. Each neuron has a long tail-like part and many branches. Neurons send messages by shooting tiny electrical currents along their tails, which connect to the branches of other neurons, thereby creating a pathway.

Neural pathways are a bit like muscles in the sense that the more you use them, the stronger they get. Each time you repeat a message, the pathway of that message gets stronger and faster – a bit like how, if you take the same route across a field again and again, your feet will gradually wear a path into the grass. And the more you take the same route, the less you will think about it – pretty soon you'll walk from one side of the field to the other without giving it a second's thought, creating a well-trodden highway in the process.

The same thing is happening as you clean your teeth each day. I am guessing as you do it, you are not thinking, "Up, down, up, down, spit, move to the back, move to the front, spit." That's because you have created a neural pathway in your brain allowing you to clean your teeth without giving it a second's conscious thought. It is how we walk, talk, eat, breathe. Our brain has created a programme that has tracked our habitual behaviour and made it easy for us by short-cutting the process. This has been very useful for human evolution, because it allows us to do lots of things on autopilot, saving our brain energy for more exciting stuff.

The problem is, your brain doesn't know the difference between healthy and unhealthy programming.

If, when you were young, you regularly had the thought, "I am not confident," your brain would create a neural 'superhighway' for that too. So, by the time you are 14 and asked to present in front of the class, you don't even have to think "I am not confident"; your brain will have already done the work for you and reflexively produced the response of fear and anxiety. That feeling then drives the behaviour (nervous, anxious) which confirms your belief that you are not good at public speaking. It's the perfect self-reinforcing loop.

The life-changing news is that you can change it.

Remember the well-trodden path through the grass? Imagine that, one day, someone points out that if you took a different route across the field, you would get home in half the time. So, the next day you take the new route. At first it is a bit tricky because no one has taken this route before; the grass is high, and it takes a bit of energy and focus to trample it down. But, about ten days in, you notice how much easier the new path is to walk on and, after a while, you have almost forgotten the old one.

Your neural pathways, and the belief systems that run on them, work in just the same way. You can decide to ignore the ones you don't want and create new ones that serve you better. Neuroscientists estimate that it takes about 3–6 months to turn a new behaviour into a habit,[4] so you have to work at it, but once it's established, you're home free. What's more, you don't have to do anything with the old pathways. You don't have to fight them or give them any attention. Just ignore them and, like the grass growing over your old time-wasting route, they will eventually fade away.

> "I knew that people like me didn't move to London and pursue big careers. No one in my family had. No one. They all took local jobs, got married young and had kids. To me it just seemed like a fact... a truth. Then my company sent me on the Ivy House Master Programme, and I couldn't believe how

many limiting beliefs I had. When I was ten, I was desperate to audition for the school play but didn't because I believed I wasn't good enough. When I was seventeen, I didn't work for my A-levels because I thought I was stupid. More recently I didn't go for a promotion because, again, I thought I was too stupid. And yet, in the three months since dropping my limiting beliefs I have been promoted, moved to London, got a hot new boyfriend and negotiated a three-month sabbatical next year so I can go travelling. I wish I'd known this earlier. I have a lot of missed opportunities to make up for!"

Rowena, 28, insurance

PAUSE AND REFLECT
Are your beliefs helping or hindering you?

Before we move on, think of three beliefs you have that are already empowering you. For example, it might be something you're good at, your support network, the opportunities in front of you. Write them down.

Now think of three beliefs that may be holding you back, limiting you. Write them down too.

Take a good look at your limiting beliefs. Are you ready to let them go? It may be that you just don't need them anymore. What would happen if you released them? Or you may choose to rewrite them so they empower you instead?

Either way, just be aware that the beliefs you see the world through will shape the life you create. They are not truths but thoughts you have bought into. And if you want different results, you're going to need different thoughts.

5. Your element

Finding your element is a phrase that was made famous by the international author and educational advisor to governments Sir Ken Robinson, in his bestselling book and TED Talk *Element*. Have you ever had a day when you just lost yourself in what you were doing? When time seemed to pass without you noticing? When you found yourself pushing to be your best self, and felt energised in the process? Well, that's your element. Whether it's performing on stage, organising an event, solving a complex equation or baking a cake... again, it really doesn't matter what it is; what matters is finding what it is so that you can spend as much time as possible in that space.

You will find your element at the point at which your strengths and your passions meet, and that looks different for everyone.

Blair had a talent for deal-making, building quick relationships with strangers and data analysis. Knowing this led him to a career in banking. The truth was he had no passion for banking. His real passion was sport. What he really wanted to do was combine his talents in deal-making, relationship-building and data analysis with his passion for sport. This realisation led him to look for opportunities in sports sponsorship and now he's on the path to a passionate, purpose-filled career.

Clearly, it's not going to be this straightforward for everyone. Not everyone who loves sport will end up working in it. But understanding what exactly it is you love about sport can help you find a job you love in another industry.

Hannah also loved sport, but when she thought about it she realised that it was the team atmosphere, challenge and competition she really loved. When she combined that with her talent for solving complex problems and leading others, she found her perfect job in pharmaceutical research, leading teams of people to create life-saving drugs.

Katherine had many strengths. She had a passion for understanding how the body worked, how nutrition could be used as fuel and how we might all maintain the health we are all born with. She had a talent for moving her body and was a born competitor – she loved to set herself goals and see herself progress. She was also a 'people person', finding it easy to communicate and connect with others. The problem was no one had ever suggested she get to know herself in this way, so she had been following career paths that seemed to make sense but left her cold. She tried being a teacher and a journalist, and while she was good at both, she knew they weren't right. Finally, she connected with who she was meant to be and is now a phenomenal yoga teacher, massage therapist and meditation guide.

So you may need to experiment to find the exact recipe that works. Let's look at one more example.

Faiza had a passion for law. She was fascinated by the history of it, how it was created and the different systems of law operating across the world. She also had a real talent for performing and everyone thought they had hit the nail on the head when they suggested she train to become a barrister, a path she willingly followed. But, when she got there, she found that while she loved 'performing' in court and figuring out the complexities of the case, she hated the business side of being a barrister and really didn't enjoy dealing with some of her clients. Because she was alert to finding her element and paid good attention to what she really loved, she finally realised that she actually wanted to become a lecturer – specifically, an expert in different legal structures and how they co-exist. She has since written two books and has a thriving consulting practice, as well as being a successful lecturer.

The really interesting thing about Faiza's journey is that her time as a barrister made her a far better lecturer and consultant. She doesn't regret it for a moment. She is just glad that she was alert to finding her element and was able to shift direction when she realised she was in the wrong place.

Because here's the thing: finding your element is not as simple as typing a question into a search engine. It requires you to be alert to what you are loving and what you're not. And it means trying things. Lots of things. And being okay with the fact that some of them won't be right for you.

I had no idea that I had a passion for human development until my brother, an accountant at the time, went on a training course. The next weekend we were both visiting my mum and, fired up by what he had learnt, he took me through the whole course he had just been on. That was over 30 years ago and I can still remember where we were sitting, the colour of the files he was using and how I felt. Excited, awake, with a thousand questions running through my head. It's exactly these kinds of feelings we need to be alert to – the kind of feelings that show us what's right for us. I find it scary to think that that breakthrough conversation with my brother could so easily not have happened if I hadn't been open to listening to him.

How do you find your element?

Pretty much all of us have grown up in this 'instant fix society'. If there's a problem, we Google it. If we want ramen, we Deliveroo it. If we have to pass a test, we cram in the content to get an A. But this is YOU we are talking about. Completely unique, undiscovered and complex… so don't be in a rush.

All you need to do right now is get on the journey of discovery and focus first on your strengths, and second on what you are passionate about. Remember, we find our element at the point at which our strengths and passions meet.

In terms of your strengths, simply start to notice what you're really good at. But we are not really talking about school subjects or specific job roles here; we are referring to real-life talents. On our programmes we use over 40 strengths to help people understand where their natural talents lie. They include things like:

Action taker: You make things happen. It exhilarates you to take action and get things moving.

Evidence seeker: Before you believe something, you want to analyse it and see the data. You love to prove or disprove ideas and facts.

Organiser: You love organising things and are happy managing lots of people and details to get things arranged perfectly.

Flexer: You enjoy change and being flexible. Adapting to new situations or circumstances is fun.

Ethical guider: People look to you for what is right and wrong because of your strong sense of values. Your life and work must be meaningful to you or you can't do it.

Storyteller: You can't help but turn your experiences into stories through words, images and sounds. The way you tell stories engages and inspires others.

Competitor: You want to compare your performance to others', and you want to win. Winning gives you the drive to be the best you can be.

Of course, there are lots more, but we also encourage people to come up with their own. Over the years, some of our alumni have come up with talents such as Institution Builder, Coastal Protector, Positive Agitator and People Matcher. These may make no sense to you, but they feel just right to the people who invented them, so don't confine yourself. Use this as an opportunity to understand yourself as deeply as you dare.

And again, ask others what natural talents they see in you. Often our talents feel so natural to us that we don't even see them as talents. My daughter Lara is a complete natural with people. Since being able to walk and talk she has always had the ability to walk into a group of strangers, say, "Hi, I'm Lara. What's your name?" and then chat to them, asking them lots of questions about themselves and sharing stuff about herself. Lara wouldn't see this as a talent because, to her, it's just who she is. It took her family to point out to her that it's actually a real strength. What talents do your family and friends see in you that you don't?

Now, having come up with a list of your strengths, start to notice what you're really interested in. If you had all the free time and money in the world, what would you spend your days doing, learning, talking and reading about? If you are struggling to get past Netflix or eyelash extensions, ask yourself what it is you love about the shows you watch, or what gets you excited about the beauty world. After all, in 2013 Essex mental health worker Michelle Lauren launched a fake-eyelash business that now turns over £100,000 a year and ships around the world. Or perhaps it's time to broaden your horizons. It can feel hard to try new things, but wouldn't it be awful if you missed your true vocation simply because you couldn't be bothered to try out that life drawing class, or gone to see that documentary on human rights?

Having gathered some ideas about where your strengths lie AND what you are passionate about, talk to everyone you know, and the people they know, about where you could combine those things. Remember: you may have a number of passions and some will always be hobbies. What you are looking for are passions that could combine well with your strengths to find a career you will love.

PAUSE AND REFLECT

What are your strengths and passions?

What could you do now to increase your understanding of your passions and strengths?

Who could you ask?

Think of as many people as you can, the more surprising the better.

6. Purpose

Feeling a sense of purpose in your life might sound like a nice optional extra, but science shows that it's much more important than that. "There have been a number of studies suggesting that a higher sense of purpose in life is associated with reduced risk of early death," says Eric S. Kim, PhD, a research scientist in the Department of Social and Behavioral Sciences at the Harvard T.H. Chan School of Public Health.[5]

Just look at David Attenborough, who is, as I write this, 92 and still making incredible wildlife programmes. Or think of the Brazilian footballer Rafinha, who grew up in poverty and then had to deal with the unexpected death of his father just after he was called up to the Brazil U17 team. His sense of purpose was what pulled him through adversity and tragedy: "I only feel complete and successful in football."

You might be allergic to cats and have two left feet, but I can tell you now you have a purpose just as powerful and valuable as theirs. Everyone has a purpose, whether they bother to find it and follow it or not. It is our reason for being, the unique contribution each of us is capable of bringing to the world. When you find your purpose, life just seems to make sense, and things seem to fall into place. You have something to live for, something that truly engages you, something you would fight to have in your life.

Some people have world-changing purposes – to stop climate change, campaign for trans rights, reform the electoral system. Others have purposes that are far simpler but just as important – to make sure their pupils leave school confident in maths, to raise healthy, happy children, or to care for the elderly in their community. All are equally valid; the important thing is to know that we all need and deserve a life of purpose.

So how do you find it?

Some lucky people just know. They've always known what they are here to do. For others, however, like me, it takes a bit longer. For those people, the vast majority of us, start with finding your element. Your purpose will be smack bang in the middle of your element. As I have shared, my journey to finding my element began when my brother shared the self-development programme he had been on. In that moment I began to nurture a lifelong passion for helping people live their best lives and combine it with my strengths to train, coach and speak to large audiences. As a result, I spent years working in my element, running my first company, travelling the world coaching senior leaders and speaking at conferences. It wasn't until I was 46, however, that I actually discovered my purpose. I realised that, while I loved what I was doing, the thing I was really passionate about was taking this transformational learning to people far earlier in their lives. I noticed how, almost on a daily basis, I got angry and frustrated about the fact that these skills that could literally change the outcome of your life were only available to a tiny percentage of the highest-paid senior executives. Over weeks and months this voice got louder and louder in my head until I finally listened, sold our business and started Ivy House. I now live a life of purpose, on a mission to bring game-changing leadership and life skills to the heart of how we develop each generation. It is my dream that this learning is available to anyone who is ready to lead their life.

So, the answer to how you find your purpose comes in two parts – find your element and stay alert. The longer you live and work in your element, the deeper you go, the clearer your purpose will become. You will begin to notice your energy being drawn in one particular direction, certain questions will keep popping into your head, you will lose yourself in learning about something new, and you will start boring your friends about it because you won't stop talking about it. Stay alert to all these signs. And, when you notice them, explore further – be prepared to try new things and eventually you'll find it.

Most of us aren't aware of or can't articulate our purpose, but I wholly believe it is innate within us, just waiting to be discovered and nurtured.

PAUSE AND REFLECT

Starting the journey of discovering your purpose

Let yourself be still and quiet for a moment. Close your eyes and take a few deep breaths.

Having stilled yourself, ask yourself if you have any inkling about what your purpose might be.

Just sit and breathe – count your breaths in and out and see what shows up. It may be nothing, which is fine, or you may just get a sense of what it might be. Just sit with it. Notice it, and in a few weeks, repeat the exercise. Learning to tune into the messages our mind and body give us is time well spent for all of us.

Finding your Core Strength will change your life

I may sound like one of those "this one trick will transform your life!" adverts on Facebook, but when it comes to Core Strength, this statement really is true. And you don't have to spend a penny on a product or video or course, because everything you need is inside you. When you know your vision for the life you want to create, what your priority driving force is, what your non-negotiable values are, which of your beliefs you want to take forward into your future, what puts you in your element and how to start looking for your purpose, you have the blueprint for YOUR one, unique, extraordinary life.

And when you have this kind of clarity, two things start to happen.

1. Success comes a whole lot easier

This means success in *all* its forms. When you know what matters to you and how to articulate it, people begin to understand you better. When you understand that everyone's core is different, you become interested in learning more about other people too. In turn, this will improve the quality of your relationships. When you're doing work you love, you put in more effort, get better at it, get recognised for it and get powerful results. All of this has a huge impact on how we feel about ourselves. When we're living a life aligned to our Core Strength, it's easier to belong, feel valued and experience unshakeable self-worth, whatever the world might throw our way.

2. You know how to rebalance

Remember: living from Core Strength doesn't mean that your future is going to be all unicorns and rainbows. What it does mean, however, is that whenever you notice that you're out of balance, you literally have a checklist to run through and find out what's wrong. Are you violating a value? Are you spending enough time in your element? Are you getting some of your driving forces met in a negative way? You now have a clear and reliable way of identifying the issue – which means you'll know exactly what you have to do to realign.

I could tell you story after story about why living from your Core Strength will make a transformative difference to your life. It honestly is the real deal. I know, because I live from it every day - and although my life isn't perfect or easy, I promise you it's bigger, braver and more meaningful than I could have ever imagined when I was starting out. What I can't do, though, is find it for you, or nag you into doing what it takes to find it yourself.

That's your call. And that requires you taking 100% ownership for your life... which is where we're headed next.

RECAP

Core Strength

Our Core Strength is our personal blueprint for our extraordinary life, made up of our vision, our driving forces, our values, our beliefs, our element and our purpose.

- Having a clear vision of what we want our life to look like and who we want to be means we can make the decisions and take the actions that will get us there.

- Driving forces underpin all our behaviour, we get to choose whether these needs are met positively or negatively, and when we understand our current priority, we can make decisions accordingly.

- Understanding the values that matter most to us enables us to make values-based decisions and create the life we truly want.

- By shining a light on the beliefs 'lens' we see the world through, we can choose which ones to keep and which ones to let go of.

- Once we find what put us in our element, we can start to figure out a career or lifestyle that we will love.

- By spending enough time in our element and staying alert, we will find our purpose.

- Life is always going to be full of challenge and change but, when we live from our Core Strength, we're able to constantly realign – understanding why we are out of balance and doing what we need to get back on track.

P.S.: In case you're curious… Sanjay did quit his job and now travels the world taking photographs for travel magazines and newspapers. He and his wife are still together, and while it was really tough in the beginning, they have found a way to make it work for both them and the boys. As he is away so much, his wife has decided to go back to university - and says she's never been happier.

And Nick is currently studying maths at a top university. After a fair amount of ribbing, he is welcome in his local anytime he's home. His dad did initially get very upset when Nick told him his plan, taking it as a personal rejection, but Nick realised this had nothing to do with him and everything to do with the beliefs his dad was holding on to. In his second year of uni, his dad came up for the weekend and apologised. They now spend loads of time together and occasionally his dad boasts about how well Nick is doing to his mates.

100% Ownership

"You only live once, but if you do it right, once is enough."
Mae West

Every one of us dreams of being free. Free to live the life we want, free to be the person we want to be, free to think and do whatever we want. So, if that's what we all want, why do so few of us have it? Why are so many people trapped in jobs they don't like, relationships that don't work, living lives that are far less than they dream of?

The OECD Better Life Index is a global project that analyses data from 36 countries in order to evaluate quality of life across the world. In 2019, when asked to rate their general satisfaction with life on a scale from 0 to 10, people on average gave it a 6.5. Even in the UK, where we rank above the average in areas including personal security, environmental quality, health status, education and skills, and income and wealth, people gave their life satisfaction an average score of 6.8.[6]

Not exactly dream-worthy, right? So what's stopping us from creating extraordinary lives?

I am about to share with you the most important equation of all time – one which you've probably never heard of.

$$E+B=R$$

Any ideas? It stands for Event + Behaviour = Result, and it is going to change your life… but only if you want it to.

There was a point in my life when two companies I worked for went out of business one after the other. It was the 1980s, when I happened to be working in the travel industry in the midst of a travel industry crisis. Finding myself unemployed, I took the opportunity to go back to university and studied for two postgraduate qualifications, both in marketing. One night, a guest lecturer from a big London agency came to speak. Excited, I sat in the front and asked lots of questions, and then when the lecture was over, I followed him into the lobby and asked if I could buy him a drink in exchange for some advice. I told him about a job I was applying for in London, then asked him if he knew the agency and could give me any tips for the interview. "Better than that," he said. "I know the MD, he's a great friend of mine. I'll call him in the morning and tell him you are one of the best students on the programme." He did this after having known me for just a few hours. Two weeks later I was offered the job.

Here's the interesting thing about this story. I could have chosen to not do any of those things. Or, I could have done exactly what I did – and the agency bigwig could have told me he was too busy to talk. One thing's for sure, though: if I hadn't tried, I would never have known.

This story demonstrates the equation (I like to call it the Extraordinary Equation) in action. The guest lecturer coming down to my university was the E, or event. Me sitting in the front, asking questions and asking him for advice was the B, my behaviour in response to that event. And the R? The result was me getting the job I wanted out of over 800 applicants.

EVENT + BEHAVIOUR = RESULT

What most people don't realise is that life is just a series of events. Your bus is late, you get the promotion, your parents get divorced, the exam question wasn't what you hoped for, your boss shows up in a bad mood, or a guest lecturer from a London agency visits your course. Most of these events, you have no control over. But how you *respond* to each of these events is completely down to you – which in turn will determine the results you get in life.

There's a second part to this story. Obviously, I had to go for an interview to get the job. Two, in fact. At the end of the first interview, with a pretty frightening female director of the company, I asked for feedback – specifically, whether she was going to put me forward for a second interview. She told me that I had done very well and she wanted to put me forward, but that my red skirt was far too short and bright to be taken seriously as a consultant and, if I wanted the job, I would need a new suit. She didn't sugar-coat the feedback – she just gave it to me straight. She was so direct I almost felt like she was angry with me. But rather than pushing back defensively, I just thanked her and went straight out and bought a longer navy suit. Once again, I was faced with a series of events and I had a choice about how to react. The first event was the end of the interview – I had a choice about asking for feedback or not. If I hadn't asked I would never have known that the length and colour of my skirt could have been the one thing standing in the way of my dream job. The second event was the nature and tone of the feedback; I could have been upset or outraged at her bluntness or riled at the conformist patriarchal business world that would underestimate a woman in a short red skirt. But, that is not where I chose to focus my energy. That was the world I wanted to succeed in, and I was willing to take ownership of that decision even if it meant being flexible in the way I dressed. That feedback changed my life and I will forever be grateful to Kay, who had the courage to give it to me.

It often feels as if life is completely out of our control, sweeping us along on waves of good or bad luck. But if we look very carefully, we see there is a gap between ourselves and each event unfolding before us, and in that gap, we get to make a choice. Those choices create our lives.

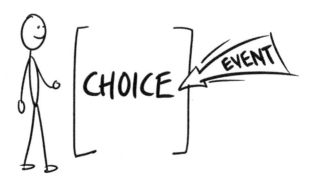

100% Ownership – what is it?

100% Ownership is about taking complete responsibility for our lives and what they become. It means knowing we have a choice in how we respond to each and every event, and understanding that our choices will create our life.

Why is it so important?

Choice is the ultimate human superpower. All other animals act from instinct, however sophisticated and well evolved, but humans have the unique ability to use their brains to choose how their lives pan out. As the legendary author and coach Stephen Covey always used to say, to be human is to take *'response-ability'*, i.e. to use our *ability* to choose our *response*. We can't always change the situation around us, but we can always choose how we react – and in doing this we get to influence the outcome in every situation we are involved in. That's an extraordinary degree of power.

Imagine for a minute that your partner, your flatmate, your mum or whoever you live with comes into your room one morning really upset about the mess you left in the kitchen. That is the event. Now, let's look at the different behaviours you could choose in response.

EVENT	+ BEHAVIOUR	= RESULT
They come into your room upset with you	You shout back and tell them to get out of your room	Tension / mutual upset / perhaps an argument
They come into your room upset with you	You ignore them and turn over in bed	Tension / mutual upset / perhaps an argument
They come into your room upset with you	You sit up, genuinely apologise, and say you will get up and tidy it up	☺

For each event that unfolds in your life, you can choose from a vast buffet of behaviours. You can flip out, get stressed, withdraw, blame someone, ignore someone, pretend to be okay when you're not, get aggressive… whatever you want. That is your human right. But the point – the REALLY IMPORTANT POINT – is that the behaviour you choose is your choice.

Which means you have the power to change the result you get. Every time.

The frightening thing is while most people seem to understand this on an intellectual level, it's not how they live their lives. When I ask the question "are exams stressful?", over 80% of people usually say yes. What they're really saying is they believe that the exams (an event) determine, or even dictate, their response: their behaviour. But that is simply not true. I know this because the other 20% have a whole range of reactions from enjoying the challenge through to being so laid back they hardly know what time the exam starts. Whenever you believe your response to any event is inevitable, you are giving up your ultimate human power – the power to choose. In other words, you are living 'outside-in' – believing that the choices you make are out of your control instead of completely down to you (inside-out).

That's why the Extraordinary Equation is so essential. It gives you back control of your future, which makes it a skill that will change your life.

PAUSE AND REFLECT

How much ownership are you taking?

Think about a time recently when you reacted to something in a way you regretted. Maybe you shouted at someone, ignored someone, chose to watch YouTube instead of working, drank too much, sent an angry text... anything.

Now consider all the other behaviours you could have chosen in the moment. How different might the results have been?

Team rhino vs team cow

The extent to which you are using the E + B = R, the Extraordinary Equation is the extent to which you are truly leading your life. Leading, as in taking control and deciding how you want it to turn out.

People who live extraordinary lives do exactly this. They're like rhinos – driving forward, consciously choosing their response. If something isn't working, they find out why and do something about it. If a relationship isn't going so well, they do all they can to fix it; and if it doesn't work, they move on. If a job isn't right, they find another one. If they get ill, they do what they can to get well. On the other hand, many, many people live their lives like cows, blindly following the herd, doing what is expected, putting up with work, relationships and a feeling of self-worth that is so much less than it could be. Sometimes unconsciously, they believe the quality of their life is determined by other people. They are experts at playing the victim, blaming one person or situation after the other for living a substandard life. They make excuses, or just wait and hope that one day they will wake up and find that happiness, meaning and success have landed in their laps.[7]

Climbing the Ownership Ladder

Is there something in your life that you're not happy with at the moment? Perhaps you feel overworked, you're in a relationship that isn't going well, you're tired and unfit, or you simply have a sense of vague dissatisfaction and lack of direction? Now ask yourself, where are you sitting on the Ownership Ladder[8] in relation to this issue?

Are you right at the bottom, claiming you didn't know about something crucial, or blaming someone or something for what happened? Are you making excuses about your time, resources or ability so you don't actually have to take action? Perhaps you are using the 'wait and hope' strategy, telling yourself if you wait long enough hopefully the situation will change of its own accord?

Or maybe, just maybe, you're taking a bit more ownership and responsibility. You've acknowledged the reality of your situation and the influence you have over it (e.g. you're unfit so decide to start exercising). The true rhinos amongst you will be at the top of the ladder and taking action (running shoes donned, you'll already be out the door).

Be 100% honest: where are you right now on the ladder?

Jack had been a star pupil all his academic career and then, for some reason, he flunked his degree. When I met with him, he was way down the ownership ladder. Apparently, he and his girlfriend had argued the night before his main exam and he'd got no sleep. His course tutor had gone off on maternity leave and the replacement was no good. The questions on the paper were unfair and he hadn't felt well on the day. Whether or not all of this was true was irrelevant. What was interesting was how Jack had chosen to respond to the 'event' of flunking his degree. He had decided not to resit the exam or take the good job he had been offered by a family friend. Instead, he had either lain in his room at home or gone out drinking with his mates most nights for months. He was angry and rude to his parents and had broken up with his girlfriend.

When we met, I told him his response was totally up to him. But, before he made his decision, he should probably know about the Extraordinary Equation and Ownership Ladder. We talked about E + B = R, and he reluctantly agreed he didn't really like the results he was currently creating in his life. He regretted the state of his relationships and the fact that he had wasted months doing nothing positive to move him forward.

When we looked at the Ownership Ladder, he realised immediately he was 'blaming others'. But what was also interesting was that he admitted that he quite liked it there. "As long as I am angry with everyone and everything else for what has happened, it saves me from having to take responsibility for my life," he said. And, I have to tell you, he hit the nail right on the head.

I can't tell you how many people I have met who love blaming others for their unhappiness. They blame their parents for getting divorced, their friends for being unkind, the economy for stopping them from getting a job, their dress size for preventing them from finding love… I could go on and on.

But the thing about ownership is that it takes guts. It requires you to find the courage to step away from the herd, to stop hiding behind the label of victim, to stand up and be counted as the leader of your life. It is SO much easier to blame others, find excuses, wait and hope things change. These are behaviours we see around us all the time. They are comfortable, familiar behaviours that can in many cases get us fleeting connection and sympathy. But they are not behaviours that lead to a bigger, braver, more meaningful life.

How to take 100% Ownership

Making the commitment to take 100% Ownership will change every part of your life. Let's start.

1. Decide who you want to be

Imagine that you're looking at a room full of people that know you. Some of these people know you really well, like your family and close friends. Others are more like acquaintances, but they've still met you at least once or twice. You're outside of the room – they can't see you – but you can hear everything they say. And they're all talking, with breath-taking honesty, about what they think you're like. Listen. What are they saying? What positive words are they using? What negative ones? Be courageous, both with the good stuff and the not so good. Jot *all* the words down.

Now take a really good look at this list, because it describes who you are in the world. You may think that deep down you are someone completely different, but this list of words is how people actually experience you, day to day. If they experience you as kind, thoughtful, fun and energetic, it's because you regularly choose these kinds of behaviours. If they describe you as grumpy, negative, two-faced or flaky, it's because you regularly choose these behaviours. It's that simple. What you choose to do, how you choose to behave, is who you are.

Rob was 32 when he came on one of our programmes. He had been struggling to get noticed in work even though he said he was working really hard. He told me he felt invisible and completely undervalued. He said, "I'm always polite and nice, I don't complain or create dramas, but every time there's a promotion, my name isn't even mentioned." While Rob seemed a bit low about this, he was also very keen to do something about it, so I suggested he did a bit of detective work. I asked him to go out to everyone he knew, and some people he didn't, and ask them to tell him the words, both positive and negative, they would use to describe him if he wasn't in the room. It was a brave thing to do. It was a rhino thing to do. And this is the summary of what came back:

Positive: Reliable. Conscientious. Loyal. Calm. Kind.

Negative: Bland. Too private. Too quiet. Boring. Timid. Inconsequential.

Clearly, Rob had a choice as to how he could respond to this information (after all, getting the information was just an event). He could slide right down the Ownership Ladder and blame others for not understanding him, not getting to know him or being mean. Or, he could thank them wholeheartedly and get to work on changing how people experienced him. Thankfully, he chose the latter.

First, he spent time thinking really deeply about who he wanted to be. Then, he came up with a list of words that people might use to describe him if he started to choose different behaviours. Not fantasy words that didn't relate to who he was at his core, but words that described the authentic inner traits he wanted people to experience. Finally, he started to behave in a way that reflected a bigger, braver Rob.

I suspect that many of you are cringing right now, saying, "I could never do that" – and you may choose to use that excuse. But here's what we know: most people are incredibly supportive when others want to develop themselves and change their behaviour. They understand the courage it takes to be vulnerable; they admire you for it, and they will go out of their way to help you.

PAUSE AND REFLECT
Start owning your behaviour

Take a moment before you move on and write down the names of three people you are close to.

Now, next to their names write the five behaviours they would say you choose most often with them.

Based on what you have written, are there any different choices you want to make?

2. Create a vision and keep it alive

We've discussed the importance of having a vision in Core Strength. Here's how you take ownership for making that happen.

Create one

If you truly want an extraordinary life, you're going to need a vision. This doesn't mean you need to have your whole life mapped out ahead of you. You don't. But you do need to have a sense of direction. So, write down what you've discovered about your vision so far and decide which areas you want to think about and explore more. You may know lots about the kind of career you want but are still undecided about whether or not you want a family. Just go back to those questions, stay curious, and keep filling in the gaps. Where do you want to go? What do you want to experience? Who do you want to meet? What do you want to get really good at? What do you want to achieve? How do you want people to experience you? Try to build a detailed picture you feel incredibly excited about. Don't force yourself to answer questions you're not ready to answer – it's fine to keep them open but do build up as much of a picture as you can.

Keep it alive

Then, choose a time, once a month or once every two months, to sit and review how you're doing. Is this vision still right for you? Are there things you want to add or take away? What's been inspiring you recently? What more have you learnt about yourself that you may need to consider? Having done that, now look at how much closer you've got to your vision. Are you actively moving in the direction of your dreams? Are you on track? Have you got distracted? Is there anyone else you can engage to help you stick to beliefs and behaviours that will get you there?

3. Take action

Save the excuses. It's not about 'having' time, it's about making time. People who live extraordinary lives make things happen. They are at the top of the Ownership Ladder – they don't just talk about things, they do things. And, they don't wait until the stars are aligned before they take action. If an opportunity arises, they take the shot.

Hugh, 17, was considering applying for a law degree. One afternoon he was asked to give a tour of his boarding school to a pair of prospective parents from Singapore. As he showed them around he shared that his family also lived in Singapore, although he'd been born in Jersey. The parents he was showing around laughed, the wife had also been born in Jersey! They continued chatting, and he went on to discover that she was a lawyer. Feeling they'd made a connection, Hugh swallowed his nerves and asked if there was any chance of gaining some work experience during the holidays. The mother happily gave him her business card and told him to get in touch.

Sally's company was struggling, and her role had been put at risk, like many of her colleagues. Instead of seeing this as a reason to get depressed and worried, she used it as an opportunity to finally stop coasting and find her ideal role. Over the next week, she invested time in finding her element, thinking about what she loved to do and asking her family and friends to contribute their thoughts. Then she decided to contact everyone she knew in the industry, tell them she was looking for her perfect role and asking whether they could help. Within a month, Sally was offered her dream job, with a pay rise, in her current company. The minute she opened up to them about what she was really passionate about, they found her exactly the right opportunity.

Making things happen sometimes means changing some pretty deep-rooted habits, which can feel challenging, but here are five things I've seen people do that really work.

1. **Ask for help.** Even from people you don't know or find scary. You'd be amazed how many people are prepared to help when asked. And if they say no, that's fine. You're no worse off than before you asked. Don't take it personally, they may have a genuine reason not to be able to offer their help right now.

2. **Bounce back.** Learn to see rejection as part of the game of life. Remember, the more times you try something, the more chances you have of success. Sylvester Stallone spent years trying to make it as an actor, with no luck. When he wrote *Rocky*, with the intention of starring in it, producers offered him $1 million to *not* be in it. Even though he was broke, he stuck by his dream of being an actor and accepted a far lower sum to be in it. To date, his movies have grossed $1.7 billion worldwide.

3. **Get good.** Your plan will probably require you to learn some skills you don't currently have. They may be technical skills, like running a set of accounts, or human skills, like building great relationships. Either way, recognising you're not the finished article, getting good at things that will get you closer to your vision, is important.

4. **Rewrite or drop your limiting beliefs.** People love hanging on to their limiting beliefs because they give them an excuse not to act. Having the courage to see your single most powerful limiting belief for what it is, and leaving it behind, could well be the catalyst for change you need.

5. **Love yourself even when you get it wrong.** SO many people struggle with the fact that they're not perfect. While intellectually they get it, in reality they spend hours beating themselves up

when they expose any vulnerability or failure to the world. All this does is waste time, take up loads of emotional energy, and keep you at the bottom of the Ownership Ladder. Let it go.

PAUSE AND REFLECT

What's stopping you?

Is there a situation in your life that you'd like to change but you're not acting on it?

What excuse/s are you using that are keeping you stuck?

How would your life be different if you made this change?

Are you ready to see the excuses for what they are and take ownership for positive change?

What change could you make today that would move you closer to what you want?

Are you going to do it?

RECAP
100% Ownership

- Life is just a series of events.

- How we respond to each event creates the quality of our life: think $E + B = R$.

- If you want to let life happen to you – channel your inner cow, blame others and follow the herd. If you want an extraordinary life, access your inner rhino: drive forward and make things happen.

- Whenever you're unhappy with something in your life, look at where you are on the Ownership Ladder and ask what you can do to climb the rungs.

- The only way others know you is through your behaviour. It's up to you to decide who you want to be and to then choose the behaviour that reflects this.

- Take ownership for developing your vision, review it regularly, and keep tabs on whether your actions are moving you towards or away from it.

- Don't beat yourself up for not being perfect. Instead, ask for help, keep trying, bounce back from rejection, learn some new skills and rewrite those beliefs that are holding you back.

- Nothing changes until you take action.

Conscious Mind

"Nothing is good or bad but thinking makes it so."
William Shakespeare

Will was late. I had already been waiting 15 minutes for him to show up to our coaching session when the door banged open and he stormed in. He was fuming. I had never seen anyone so angry. He had just come out of an exam and it had been 'a disaster'. His 'idiot' of an English teacher had taught them the wrong Chaucer text. "I mean how can that even happen?" he raged. "How did no one notice? He'd better not show up here or God knows what I'll do to him. There's no way I will get into my first choice of uni now. Oh my God, I can't believe it. My life is ruined."

I sat watching, wondering how this would play out. As soon as he got hold of his parents (he had tried them both numerous times) I had no doubt that they too would get angry. Summon the headteacher, make lots of calls and lots of threats and probably have days, if not weeks, of stress.

When they hear this story, most people completely get Will's response. They think, "Well, fair enough. His reaction is completely justified. I'd feel exactly the same. His life may well be ruined!"

But what if all that anger, fear and frustration didn't come from 'The Chaucer Incident' at all? What if all those feelings were totally self-created, by Will, his mum, his dad and the head? What if this was actually just an event, rather than a disaster?

Remember this equation?

$$E + B = R$$

That's right: Event + Behaviour = Result. The Chaucer Incident was the event, something out of Will's control, but the behaviour, that was totally down to Will. And the behaviour he chose resulted in him having a really bad few weeks. He spent those weeks obsessing over thoughts of his life being ruined, stressing about what he could possibly do and imagining how he could get back at his teacher.

Will didn't know he was choosing his behaviour. To him, it felt a completely natural reaction. And in some ways it was. It was habitual, automatic. But the event, however shocking, didn't 'demand' that reaction. Will could've chosen to respond in many different ways. It's just that, in that moment, he chose to believe that $E = B$; that his behaviour was an inevitable result of what had happened. He chose to live outside-in.

Of course, I had a lot of sympathy for Will. I got it. We've all been in situations where our behaviour feels like it's being driven by what's going on around us. Someone shouts at us and we shout back – their fault for making us angry, right? Our boss gives us a ton of work and we spiral into stress – their fault for piling so much on our plate, right? Wrong. It might sound hard (and it is), but if we want to live an extraordinary life, then we need to take back our ultimate power – the power of choice.

To do that – to get ourselves in a position where we are able to choose our reaction – we need to understand what drives our behaviour in the first place. And that means learning the skill of Conscious Mind.

Conscious Mind – what is it?

Conscious Mind is the skill of being in a state of deep awareness. Aware that you are not your thoughts. Aware that thoughts come in and out of your head constantly, but it's your choice what to do with them – hold on to them and let them overpower you or let them go so they don't affect you at all. Accessing your Conscious Mind gives you the power of choice. The ultimate human power to choose our response to anything that comes our way.

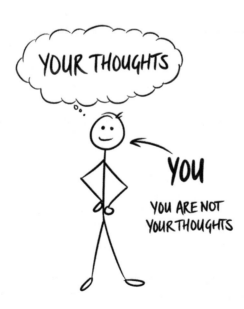

Why is it so important?

The thoughts you choose to focus on determine how you feel, and how you feel directly affects the quality of your life. Spend your day constantly focusing on negative thinking and you will have a bad day. Alternatively, deciding not to get caught up in that negative thinking and choosing to hang out with more positive thoughts will mean you'll have a better day. Truly, the choice is yours.

To develop the skill of Conscious Mind, there are three things you need to know.

First: Thoughts are random

Have you ever had a thought about really hurting someone? For a minute or two, in that moment when you were so angry you wondered how you could 'get back at them' – or at least cause them a lot of pain? Yes, me too. Does it make us bad people? No, hopefully not. Because in that moment, when we have those thoughts, we are aware they are just thoughts – we are aware we have a choice whether or not to act on that thought or not. Most of us just let the 'bad' thoughts pass through and we find a better way to deal with the situation.

According to a study from the National Science Foundation in the US, we have between 12,000 and 60,000 thoughts a day.[9] Most of them are random, and many of them totally contradictory – one minute you may have the thought, "God I love her," then ten minutes later, "God I hate her!" Which one is true? Neither? Both? Actually, it doesn't really matter. What matters is that we recognise that they are both just ideas that pop into your head. They are not truths nor facts, and we need to start seeing them as the random pieces of thinking that they are.

Earlier today, I went for a walk with the dog and, as I walked, I used the audio recorder on my phone to list the thoughts that popped into my head during the first minute. Here's a tiny extract from the final list:

I need some fresh air.

I wonder how polluted our road is.

I'm hungry.

Do we have any cake left?

Did I book those tickets?

What month are we in?

Have I got a headache?

I love spaniels.

God, Sara is annoying.

Why are there so many kinds of grass?

I need to change that slide for my presentation.

How does Viktor Frankl spell his name?

Did we put the bins out?

Oh no – was I supposed to pick Lara up from school?

Does she think I'm a rubbish mum, or does she understand? I'll ask her... have I asked her? I think I have already. What did she say?

I think my memory is going.

I really must make sure I cover trust in Intentional Relationships.

This park is so dirty.

I want some sun and some sea.

What will we have for dinner?

Do we have any cake left?

Random thought after random thought, most of which we (normally) pay no attention to whatsoever.

Second: Thinking drives behaviour – all of the time

I want you to make yourself feel angry for a moment. Go on, get angry. Do anything you need to do to make yourself feel really, really angry.

Are you angry yet?

Okay… what did you do? I'm guessing that you THOUGHT about something or someone that makes you FEEL angry. And that is how our minds work, all of the time. Our thinking drives our feelings and our feelings drive our behaviour. We call it TFB. Think – Feel – Behave.

THINK → FEEL → BEHAVE

Let's imagine you're going to a party where you don't know many people. How you THINK will determine how you FEEL, and how you FEEL will determine how you BEHAVE.

THINK	FEEL	BEHAVE
This is going to be a nightmare and so embarrassing. I am going to have to drink my way through this.	Anxious, shy, determined to get drunk to numb the anxiety.	Head straight to the bar and take three shots straight down, stand awkwardly in the corner staring at your phone, then throw up on your way home.
This should be a good laugh; it'll be nice to meet some new people; I wonder who'll be there?	Open, warm, excited, curious.	Introduce yourself to a few people, ask them about themselves and tell them about you. Have a laugh.

The thing about feelings and thoughts is that they are always attached – they are like two sides of a coin. You can't have one without the other. So, if we spend time thinking we are ugly, stupid, bored, anxious or shy, those thoughts will produce the corresponding feelings – low confidence, lack of motivation, loneliness, anxiety – and those feelings will produce the corresponding behaviours.

Just pause for a moment and consider what kind of thoughts you regularly hang onto about yourself? And when you do that, how do you feel?

At any moment in time, if you want to know why you're feeling the way you are, ask what's going on in your thoughts.

This is how it played out for Will:

Thinking: "This is the end of my life." "This is unbelievable." "Why me?" "This is SO unfair."

Feeling: Anger, outrage and fear.

Behaviour: Has a big argument with his teacher, shows lots of aggression towards his family, has very little sleep.

Quality of his life (in those few weeks): Feels he's hit rock bottom – low mood, stressed and anxious.

Instead, it could have gone this way:

Thinking: "Okay, that was unexpected." "This will affect everyone in the class." "It must have happened before; I should find out what the options are."

Feelings: Calm, proactive, curious, clear.

Behaviour: Gets in touch with his chosen university, has a really mature, brave conversation with the Head of Department, gets her to agree to consider his predicted grades, has thoughtful, considered conversations with his family, is gentle with himself and gets some early nights.

Quality of his life: Good. He feels in control and supported and is open to what may happen.

When I use this example, I usually get a response of incredulity. People say things like: 'Well, a person can't be calm all the time, sometimes there are dramas!' And they'd be right – but the point they miss is that they themselves are often creating the drama by how they choose to respond to the event.

The events in themselves do not create our feelings. We do. We choose how we are going to THINK about the event and that determines how we FEEL and BEHAVE. The problem is, most of the time, it doesn't feel that way. You might get triggered into an angry reaction by the thought, "This is unfair." If you are unaware that you've had that thought, you will naturally assume the anger has been automatically triggered by the event. But there is always something in the middle: your thinking.

In reality, the event hits your thinking, this turns into a feeling and the feeling drives the behaviour. And my oh-so-simple equation begins to look a little more complex.

$$E + (T \rightarrow F \rightarrow B) = R$$

So when 'The Chaucer Incident' happened (the event), Will chose a set of thoughts that drove a corresponding set of feelings and behaviours. Which all resulted in him having a pretty awful week. If, instead, he'd let the negative thinking just pass through him and chosen to focus on more constructive thoughts, the weeks that followed would have taken on a very different flavour.

When we develop the skill of accessing our Conscious Mind, we are able to remind ourselves on a daily basis that we get to choose. It doesn't mean that you will never have angry or frustrated thoughts again. You most certainly will. But the more you practise stepping out of your thinking and into your Conscious Mind, the easier it becomes to remember that you don't need to hold on to those thoughts if you don't want to.

The important word here is 'choose'. Of course, if you choose to build on a feeling of anger, frustration or stress, you can. No one will take that away from you. Most people, however, don't even know they have a choice; they are simply living their lives outside-in, believing that how they feel is being caused by what's going on around them, not by their own thinking. Learning the skill of Conscious Mind gives them back that choice.

Linda was an impressive woman. She had risen to a senior position in the engineering company she worked for by being super-bright, working unbelievably hard and having a knack for focusing on the areas that had the biggest impact on business success. The problem was that, while the board truly valued Linda's business acumen and her commitment, they were hesitant to move her into the senior leadership team because of her energy. What became clear is that all of them experienced her as 'stressed' most of the time. They found every conversation with her started with her telling them about the latest 'disaster' she was having to deal with and, while they were pleased she was giving it her attention, they found her draining to be around. Linda was a prime example of someone living outside-in, believing that her mood was completely determined by the latest crisis she was trying to deal with. What Linda didn't realise was that the crisis was just another event, and how she thought about it would determine both how she felt and how she behaved with others. She wasn't aware that she had other options; that she could still take the crisis seriously and work hard to resolve it but do so in a calm, considered, positive way.

Just to be clear, I'm not saying that now you know you have a choice, you'll be able to move into a state of conscious awareness at any time. If it was that easy, it wouldn't be an extraordinary skill. But I do promise you this: the more you practise the art of stepping out of your thinking and putting a bit of distance between the triggering event and your reaction to it, the easier it will become. The coaches at Ivy House have taught this for years and we still get caught up in our thinking, but it's not a big deal because as soon as we notice it, we just do something about it. And that's where the third part comes in.

Third: You can choose the thoughts you spend time with

I am about to share three steps that have changed thousands of people's lives. Steps that enable them to let anxiety pass through them, rather than take hold of them. Steps that mean they can stop obsessing and worrying about the future and, instead, remain calm and curious, knowing that whatever comes their way, they'll be able to handle it. Sound good? Here we go.

Step 1: Get over your emotophobia

Emotophobia, a word coined by the brilliant coach Michael Neill, describes the fear of emotions. If we want to feel happier, safer and more confident in our lives, the first thing we need to do is recognise that, as human beings, we feel emotions. Emotions of all kinds. Big, fat, hairy, wonderful emotions. We simply can't escape them. And we need to make them our friends.

Once we recognise that all emotions – sadness, pain, heartbreak, frustration, joy, excitement, love and belonging (to name a few) – are simply part of the deal of being human, everything becomes so much easier. The problem is that, somewhere along the line (from our parents, TV shows, self-help books, Instagram…), most of us get taught that a 'good' life is one chock-full of 'good' emotions and entirely devoid of 'bad'. That's just not realistic or even desirable. How would we know we were having a great day if we never had a grim one? So, if we're going to be strong, resilient and fully alive, we have to learn to be okay with emotions of all kinds, including the 'bad'.

Let's imagine you wake up one day with a feeling of sadness. You can't really put your finger on it; most things in your life are going okay, but for some reason you just feel sad. You could decide there and then that it's simply going to be a sad day and choose all the corresponding behaviours. You could be grumpy with your family and friends, not do the work you'd planned, and bring a low energy to everything you do.

Alternatively, you could wake up and think, "Oh! I have a feeling of sadness at the moment. That's interesting. Is there any action I need to take? Or can I just let it pass through?" Because here is the amazing thing: leave an emotion to its own devices, without trying to hold onto it, overthink it or block it, and it will pass through your body very quickly. You may well not believe that, because you've never tried it, but it's absolutely true.

It sounds mad that we should want to hold onto uncomfortable emotions, but many of us do. When we feel that 'forbidden' emotion, we tend to focus in on it and build it up into something much bigger than it was to begin with. Giving it power. It's possible, for example, to move from having a vague feeling of stress to having a full-blown panic attack within minutes. I've seen this countless times: people putting themselves in a state where they can barely function, purely through the power of thought (I've done the same myself). The thing is, thoughts are made of energy – mental energy – so it's in their nature to keep moving. If we don't grab hold of them and pile other thoughts on top of them, they'll just pass through, and your natural sense of ease will return.

The other extreme is trying to block these scary emotions. Rather than letting them pass through we try and block them – afraid of feeling the emotions of sadness, loneliness, fear or anger, we try and deny them access. Avoiding and blocking take many forms, but one of the most common is known as numbing. Numbing activities include such things as excessive eating, shopping, drugs, alcohol or social media, but the results are just as bad as overthinking our feelings. Blocking emotions doesn't make them go away. Instead, they become scratches on the lens you see the world through – blurring your vision and preventing you from engaging freely and joyfully in the world around you.

So, what's the answer?

First, you need to acknowledge and embrace the fact that feeling a whole range of emotions is inevitable and *good*. It's proof you're alive! For some of us, joy and happiness can feel just as scary as anxiety or hate. The key is to drop the fear and the judgement. From now on, all emotions are okay.

When you do experience unhelpful emotions, check in with yourself. Are these emotions a sign that something needs to be addressed or changed? If so, make an agreement with yourself to address the issue from a position of strength and positivity. If not, you've probably just grabbed hold of a random unhelpful thought. Give yourself the choice to just let it pass on and release it back into the wild.

There will be times, of course, when your uncomfortable feelings are the result of you thinking about something like a loved one getting ill, or the end of a relationship. And of course, you may well choose to think and feel sad in response to that. That's fine; it's human. But just remember that you can move on from that feeling when you are ready. Feelings can be healing. Just don't let them hold you back.

PAUSE AND REFLECT

Understanding your feelings

Are you in the habit of focusing in on certain thoughts or feelings, overthinking them, and, by doing so, creating more drama, panic, anger and stress?

Are there any emotions that you are regularly avoiding?

Emotions that are signalling the need to address something in your life?

Are you engaging in any numbing activities?

If so, which ones – and which emotions do you think you are trying to block?

Step 2: Choose which thoughts to focus on

When we learn the skill of Conscious Mind, we learn that we can choose which thoughts to give attention to and which to let pass through. As you already know, we have thousands of thoughts a day, most of them coming in and out unconsciously. At Ivy House we call them 'thought-drones' and we imagine them, buzzing around, flying in and out of our heads all day.

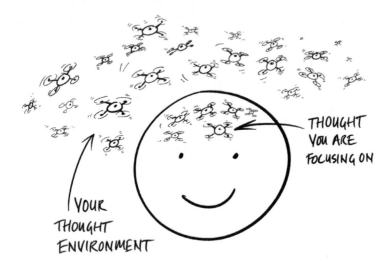

The thing is, these drones are not born equal – some drive more negative feelings and behaviour, while others create more positive feelings and behaviour. Bearing in mind we can't give them all equal time and attention, it makes sense to decide which ones we want to focus on. Remember that National Science Foundation research? As well as calculating the number of thoughts we have in a day, it found that on average around 80% of those thoughts are unhelpful, and around 95% are the same repetitive thoughts we had the day before. That means we really do have to roll up our mental sleeves and do some conscious work if we want to get different and better results in our life than we have up until now.

Imagine for a moment there is a mini you, standing in a vast dome-like room which is your mind. The space is buzzing with thought-drones, flying all around you – there are helpful drones (give them a colour) and unhelpful drones (give them a colour too). In your hand you have a net to catch hold of any drone you like, knowing when you catch it you can give it a lot of attention and make it very important. Which ones would you choose?

This is effectively what we do every day. Random thoughts fly in and out and we, usually unconsciously, choose to give all our attention to just a few. The thoughts we choose to focus on then determine the quality of our next hour, our day, our week and, ultimately, our lives.

If you need any proof of how powerful your thinking is, think back to the last time you had a bad dream. Do you remember how you felt when you woke up: riled, anxious, angry, scared? And, do you remember how, even when you knew that it was just a dream, it took you a while to calm down and feel better? That's what is going on in your mind and body every single day. You think and, as a result, you feel. You feel and, as a result, you behave. If you spend most of your time focusing on and building up unhelpful thoughts, that's going to add up to an unfulfilling life.

On hearing this, some people protest, "Well, if you never focus on the negative you will never make any changes in life." That's simply not how it works. Positive thoughts are not all about how wonderful things are – they are also about recognising that some things need to change and feeling the power to change them. Unhelpful thoughts, on the other hand, nearly always make you feel downtrodden, demotivated and disempowered.

When I met Janey, she was a nervous wreck. Her confidence was shattered, and she was exhausted both mentally and physically.

Eventually, after hours of talking, I discovered that Janey was being verbally abused by her boyfriend. That was the event. On top of this Janey then admitted to spending hours focusing on unhelpful drones. Her thinking went something like this:

"I hate him, I have to leave him… but he says it's my fault. He says I make him angry. I probably do. If I can just try to stop annoying him, it'll probably get better. If I leave him, I'm going to be on my own. And then I'll never meet anyone, and I'll be on my own forever. The thing is, I love him, and I don't want to leave him. I know he loves me really… he's just having a really bad time at the moment." And on and on.

Janey was spending nearly all day, every day, focusing on unhelpful thoughts and limiting beliefs and they were making things worse. It was only when she learnt to focus on positive, empowering thoughts such as "I deserve a loving, respectful relationship" and "I can get myself out of this situation" that she was able to make the changes she badly needed. Nothing changed until she changed her thoughts.

As we develop the skill of Conscious Mind, we learn to become aware of whether our thoughts are moving us forward or keeping us stuck. And then we get to choose which ones we want to grow.

Step 3: Become a brilliant driver AND a mechanic

Imagine for a moment that you've been given the car of your dreams but have no idea how to drive it. That car is like your mind. Your mind is the most incredible, powerful engine in the universe, but if you're going to experience the benefits, you're going to have to learn how to use it. The way to do that is by learning the skill of Conscious Mind.

Just like when you're first learning to drive, you're uncertain and hyper-vigilant. Then, about a month after passing your test, you'll notice that you've just driven from A to B without noticing what you were doing. Remember those neural pathways? Well, you've just created a new one. Driving starts to feel natural and all is going along fine until, one day, the car stops. You panic, wondering whether it's permanently broken… until the mechanic points out that you've let the petrol tank run empty.

Your mind is exactly the same. If you want to foster a Conscious Mind, you'll first need to focus on how to develop your new thinking habits. But learning how is not enough. You also need to make sure your Conscious Mind has all it needs to stay in top condition. And this means looking after your thought environment, letting go of thought spirals and putting in place a good maintenance programme – a bit like servicing that car of yours.

A healthy thought environment

The biggest influence on the nature of the thoughts that pop into our head is our thought environment: the thoughts that surround us on a daily basis.

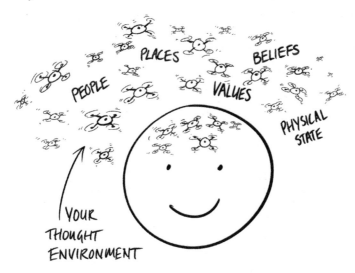

Our thought environment is made up of things like our values, our beliefs, and our physical and mental state. For example, if we have a value of equality, it will impact on what we think about the gender pay gap. If we have a belief that we are shy, it will influence what we think when asked to present in front of a group. If we have a hangover, it will massively influence how we view the day ahead of us.

It is also influenced by the people, places and cultures we spend time in. Spend all your time with friends who love to moan, and it will affect how you think. If you always get your news from the same source, read the same kind of books, or watch the same films, then your thought environment will become narrower and narrower, reflecting the nutrient-light diet you're feeding your brain.

The important point about thought environments is that you can change them. Yes, once again, you're in control. Look around you. Are you surrounded by negative thinkers or positive ones? Do you seek out a diversity of opinions, or are you bombarded by the same old ideas? Do the images you scroll through on your phone make you feel strong or fill you with self-doubt?

Step out of thought spirals

Thought spirals are those whirlwinds of thought we get into when we get lost in our thinking. We lose our perspective, become obsessive about something and lose our ability to think clearly.

Have you ever been in one? I'd be surprised if you haven't. In fact, most of us don't just have thought spirals, we have particular favourites that we like to return to time and time again. They sound something like this:

"Omg, I have so much work to do… I will never get it done on time… and I'll probably do a rubbish job anyway… Remember that time I screwed up… I'm not cut out for this… Why can't I concentrate?"

Or like this:

"Ugh, I look so fat in this... Why did I have that burger last night? I didn't need it... and I had that Twix earlier in the day... What the hell is wrong with me?... Why can't I stop eating?... No wonder no one wants to go out with me."

Or this:

"I'm so tired... What's the point in all this anyway?... I am just on a conveyer belt... It's not like anyone has ever asked me whether I want this... I'm not even going to bother getting up... I don't give a damn what they say."

Thought spirals come in all shapes and sizes: big, small, occasional and constant. They all share two characteristics, however: they are absolutely no fun and not in any way productive.

The good news is that there is another option. At any time, you can choose to step out of a spiral and into the comfy armchair of Conscious Mind.

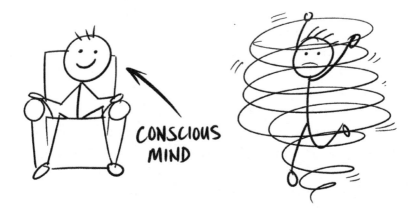

CONSCIOUS MIND

Take a look at the diagram for a moment. Where do you think is the best place to make decisions from? The spiral, caught up in the illusion that we are our thoughts? Or the armchair, with space and calm to remember that we can choose which thoughts to focus on?

From the armchair you can remind yourself that, whatever you're feeling right now is stemming from your thinking. You can take a deep breath and just notice the thoughts flying in and out. When you do this, you separate yourself from your thinking and quieten your mind. And when you quieten your mind, you get access to your real wisdom. The wisdom that sits inside you all the time. You've probably caught snatches of it, now and then, beneath all the chatter: that deep sense of knowing who you really are and what you really want.

And from this place of calm and wisdom you can decide what, if anything, needs to be done. From the comfy chair of the Conscious Mind, you can decide if you need to do anything in response to the event you are concerned about, or if you should just move on and leave that thinking behind.

Now, you might notice that, even if you've managed to move to the armchair, within just a few short minutes you jump straight back into your thought spiral. That's okay. It happens to all of us. Some thought spirals are very compelling. Just close your eyes, take a deep breath, focus on your breathing for a few minutes, and you'll be able to step back out again. You may need to go through this process once, twice or thirty times in an hour, but it doesn't matter, because the more you do it, the more you'll be exercising the muscle of Conscious Mind – and the stronger it will get. Pretty soon you'll have created a neural pathway that will allow the destructive thoughts to pass through you.

Create a good maintenance programme

The stuff you're learning here will change your life – but only if you keep practising. Sadly, it's not something you can do a few times and expect to stick. It's just like staying fit; you can't go to the gym for a month and expect your body to stay strong and trim forever more – you have to commit to going every week and, when you miss a few weeks, re-commit as soon as you can. Find the joy in the challenge and make it a part of your everyday life.

After doing this work for years at Ivy House, we've found that there are a few things that make a big difference to keeping us on track. The first is a daily meditation practice. As little as ten minutes a day will make the world of difference to your ability to separate yourself from your thinking. The second is our commitment to reading and listening to books and podcasts that help remind us of the importance of Conscious Mind. Whether we're driving, walking the dog or just lying on the sofa, immersing ourselves in this learning helps reinforce our understanding of how our feelings and thinking are connected. Finally, we commit to a regular reflection practice, where we can take the time to think about how we are doing, answer some key questions and make decisions about what we need to adjust in order to live from a healthier and more positive place.

When I met Andrew, he was at his wits' end. Whilst he loved his role as CEO of a manufacturing business, he felt he was losing his mind. Every night he had trouble switching off, and when he finally fell asleep, he often found himself awake again at 3 or 4 in the morning, his mind buzzing. He described the inside of his head as a swarming hive of bees. He said he couldn't remember when he last felt calm. What was interesting about Andrew was that about a year earlier he had spent time working with a great coach, and had begun to understand how thoughts, feelings and behaviour worked, but he had forgotten the crucial bit: you have to keep practising. You have to keep reminding yourself that you're not your thoughts and that you have a choice as to which thoughts you hang out with. During his session, Andrew made a commitment to listen to audiobooks every morning on his daily run, and to meditate for at least ten minutes every evening after work, as a way of decompressing before dinner with his family. After three days of this new routine, he rang me, told me he felt like a new man, and swore never to let these daily practices slip again.

I'll talk more about how and why meditation can help in Extraordinary Skill 6: Proactive Wellbeing, and you can find a list of recommended books at the end of this book. You can also get access to constant reminders via our Instagram @IvyHouseWorld and by following Ivy House on LinkedIn – so there's no excuse to forget!

The final step in setting up your maintenance programme is to decide *now* what you will do when you fall off the wagon. Because you will. We all do. The easy thing to do is say, "Oh well, that didn't work – I knew it wouldn't," and fall back into a world of thought spirals, sitting on the lower rungs of the Ownership Ladder and blaming everything around you for how you feel.

That, of course, is an option. It's always your choice (are you bored of me saying that yet?).

But the other option is to acknowledge that maintaining a Conscious Mind is like cleaning your teeth – stop doing it and eventually they'll fall out. But clean them twice a day, with regular flossing, and you'll be able to enjoy all the most nutritious, delicious treats that life has to offer.

Which reminds me: do we have any cake left?

RECAP

Conscious mind

- The Extraordinary Equation E + B = R shows us that we can always choose how we behave in relation to any event, however challenging that might seem in the moment.

- Conscious Mind is the skill of being aware that we are not our thoughts, accepting that thoughts are random, and understanding that we have the power to choose the ones we want to spend time with.

- Thinking always drives feeling, and feelings drive our behaviour, so if we want to take control of the kind of day we're going to have or the way we want to react to an event, we have to start by changing our thoughts.

- To take the first step towards Conscious Mind, we need to get over our emotophobia and accept that being human means we'll experience the full gamut of emotions; they're nothing to be afraid of and they'll pass through naturally if they're not overblown or blocked.

- Then we must practise choosing which thoughts we want to focus on out of the thousands of thought-drones whirring about in our heads: casting our mental net out to catch the ones that are the most strengthening and helpful to us, and letting the others go.

- We must also learn to maintain a healthy Conscious Mind over the long term by ensuring we surround ourselves with a diverse, positive thought environment; learning to step out of thought spirals when they suck us in; and regularly strengthening our mind muscles with daily meditation and inspiration.

- At any time, we can choose to separate ourselves from the chaos of our thoughts and sit back into the comfy armchair of Conscious Mind, from where we can regain our power to choose how we want to focus our energy… and determine the results we get in our lives.

Courageous Learner

"The minute that you're not learning, I believe you're dead."
Jack Nicholson

A question for you.

ARE YOU ABOVE

———————————————————————

OR BELOW THE LINE?

Which is it?

For years I've asked senior leaders this very question. I tend to work with bright people, so they understand pretty quickly that there is a 'right' and a 'wrong' place to be and, without really understanding what the question means, they often begin to plump for whichever position they believe will put them in the correct camp.

This behaviour is interesting in itself; in our experience, some people are more concerned about giving the 'right' answer, as opposed to giving the 'real' answer. They are more focused on people seeing they are right than really thinking about what's true.

I would then go on to explain the 'above/below the line' model, which is a truly powerful tool that top business leaders have been using for years (I particularly like how it's used in Jim Dethmer's book, *The 15 Commitments of Conscious Leadership*). In a nutshell, when people are above the line, they are open, curious and motivated by learning. When they are below the line, they are closed, defensive, and motivated by being right and winning.

MOTIVATED BY LEARNING

MOTIVATED BY BEING RIGHT

It best shows up in conversations. When we're having a conversation with someone who has a different opinion to us, are we more interested in learning from them or convincing them that our view is the right one?

I would then ask my leaders to decide where they normally sit when having conversations. I'd explain that it's a binary decision. At any one time, they are either above or below the line; they can't be in the middle, neither, or both. It's interesting what happens. First, there are still a group of people that choose the 'right' answer and put their hands up for 'above' the line, without any regard for whether or not it's true. Some, however, are caught by the words 'motivated by being right and winning' and sit in a contemplative silence wondering whether or not to admit that, yes, most of the time they just want to be right.

Courageous Learner – what does it mean?

Courageous Learners are motivated by learning. They take joy and satisfaction in learning about themselves, others and whatever situation they find themselves in, without the need to always be right, win, prove their worth or defend their point of view. Courageous Learners are acutely self-aware and have the ability to tell the truth to themselves and others. They proactively seek to change and develop themselves throughout their lives.

Why is it so important?

When we're motivated by being right, our priority is to protect our ego. For some reason, most of us believe that when we're wrong, it reduces our self-worth. We believe that if we don't win, we're a failure; that if we don't come top of the class, we're not as valuable as someone who did. I spent a long time believing these things when I was younger, and at the time they seemed perfectly natural; but when you think about them deeply, they are totally mad. If you operate from these beliefs, you get a world of pain and self-judgement. You end up creating relationships that become battlegrounds and leaders who are more concerned with being right than doing the right thing for the organisation. And in many ways, that's the world we find ourselves in now.

That doesn't mean that Courageous Learners are always free of ego or purely motivated by learning. They're still human, with a full range of emotions like anyone else. The truth is, neither being above the line nor below the line marks you out as a Courageous Learner. Like all of us, Courageous Learners can find themselves in either place. The difference is that they always know where they are at any one time. They are self-aware enough to know whether they're just trying to be right, and they are proactive and honest enough to do something about it.

Think for a moment about the last conversation you had that didn't go so well. Where do you think you were? Above or below the line?

Two friends, Bill and Ben, were doing the Ivy House Award. They were about to leave school and had decided to go on a gap year together. The problem was, Bill wanted to start in America and Ben in Australia. Who was right? Bill? Ben? Neither?

Whenever they began to talk about it, they lapsed into an argument, each one getting louder and more aggressive as they tried to impress their points on the other. After a while Ben simply gave in, because he was fed up with the constant conflict. But deep down, he still really wanted to start his travels in Australia. At this point he was tempted to call the whole thing off and suggest they go their own ways.

This scenario plays out in relationships and businesses time and time again, as people who are motivated by being right talk across each other, shout and roll their eyes in order to 'win'. The topic of discussion is irrelevant. What matters, and needs to change, is to stop living below the line.

When Bill and Ben began to learn about Courageous Learners on the Award, they agreed to try and explore the issue from above the line – to be curious and open, to truly listen to one another and consider each other's views. They soon understood that each of their opinions was as a result of the data they had been fed over the years: the books they'd read, the films they'd watched, the people they followed on social media, as well as the opinions of their parents, schools and the people around them.

They actually discovered that after ten years of being friends there was more to learn about each other than they'd ever imagined. And by understanding the nuances of each other's desires, they soon realised that there were lots of good reasons to start in either place. They ended up agreeing to start in America, but to then allocate extra time to linger in Australia. In other words, because they were using the skill of being Courageous Learners, they chose a different behaviour in the conversation – and got a much better result.

When people are motivated by learning, they listen, ask genuine questions and are prepared to change their minds. In fact, Courageous Learners are happy to do so, because they don't associate it with being weak. On the contrary, they see it for what it is: a strength.

MOTIVATED BY LEARNING

SHARE INFORMATION. SHARE THOUGHTS AND FEELINGS. LISTEN. COLLABORATE. WAIT FOR OTHERS TO FINISH. TALK NORMALLY. REFLECT. CONSIDER. CHANGE.

MOTIVATED BY BEING RIGHT

HOLD BACK INFORMATION. PRETEND TO LISTEN. GET LOUD OR VERY QUIET. INTERRUPT. COMPETE. TALK OVER OTHERS. AVOID CONFLICT. DECIDE BEFORE THE CONVERSATION. MANIPULATE. RESIST CHANGE.

Our cultural conditioning of being below the line has very ancient roots, from the days when sabre-toothed tigers roamed the earth. When we are below the line, we are in a primitive state of survival, flooded with hormones that narrow our thinking as our fight or flight mechanism comes into play. Today, although there are no sabre-toothed tigers, we use the exact same protection mechanism when we think our ego is being threatened. When our boss ignores us in a meeting, or our friend confronts us about something we've done wrong, our brain shrieks 'tiger!' and goes into lockdown.

Unfortunately, when we're in this state, we're good for nothing but freezing or running. Under stress, we experience a rapid loss of cognitive ability – we literally cannot think. We need tiger-free time and space for learning, listening and being creative. Once we're above the line, however, we're in a creator state. Because we feel safe, we're able to play, try out new ideas, change our minds and listen to different points of view. It's from this place that the best ideas are developed, and it's from this place that decisions should be made.

In 1978, a team of American psychologists led by a woman called Carol Dweck[10] gave a group of four-year-olds a simple jigsaw puzzle. Once they'd all completed it, the children had a choice: they could redo the puzzle they'd been given or have a go at a trickier one.

Some of the children opted to stick with the easy puzzle they'd already solved, eager to reinforce their ability and enjoy the pleasure of being right. Having been told by the researchers that clever kids don't make mistakes, they wanted to avoid the risk that they might fail. Others in the group, however, didn't care whether they messed up. They thought that repeating the same puzzle would be boring, and they relished the opportunity of a new challenge.

This seminal study marked the early days of a now-flourishing discipline: the science of mindsets. The first group of children exhibited a 'fixed mindset': a belief that their abilities had a limit, which led them to anxiously cling onto what they already knew. The second group, however, demonstrated a 'growth mindset': a belief that true success only comes from stretching yourself. Though at four years old, they couldn't understand or rationalise their responses.

Having a growth mindset has been proved to be a crucial factor in what makes the difference between people who succeed to an extraordinary level, and those who stay on a plateau. It's the hallmark of a Courageous Learner. But subsequent studies from Dweck and her followers also found that, as we get older, Courageous Learners are increasingly rare.

The challenge many of us have is that the environments in which we live and work don't always feel safe. Get something wrong in school and you fear you may be judged or punished. The same dynamic plays out at work. Even the most senior leaders worry that if they're not seen to have the right answer, it might compromise their career. And at home so many people believe getting something wrong or changing their mind will appear weak.

The problem is, the more you operate from below the line – closed, defensive, not listening, determined to be right – the more you'll become the kind of person people don't want to hang out with, live with or employ.

The good news is that we now know that our feelings and behaviour come from our thinking NOT what's going on around us. We're always in control. So, if your thinking is, "In this conversation I want to genuinely listen, share my thoughts in a respectful way, and together work out the best solution," you'll feel confident, curious and open. If on the other hand, your thinking is, "I just need to get them to agree to my idea," then you'll feel defensive, anxious and primed to shout, bully or manipulate.

PAUSE AND REFLECT

Being honest about your behaviour

Take a moment and look at the behaviours listed above and below the line.

Which behaviours do you regularly choose? Be honest.

Where do you think you usually are in a conversation? Above or below the line?

Does it depend who you're with? Have you got into the habit of being above the line or below the line with certain people, or in certain situations?

Living above the line

Mia had been good at everything for most of her life. She'd done exceptionally well in school, got a first-class degree, wore all the right clothes, hung out with the right people and was considered very attractive. So, it was a complete shock when, working in her first job as an Assistant Account Executive in a digital agency, she wasn't chosen to be part of the pitch team for Amazon's Super Bowl advert. This was THE opportunity of the year. If they won it, the company would surely go on and win an award, and the team that did it would be 'made'. How could this have happened? Even worse, how had Karim got it instead of her? She went home raging: yelled at her boyfriend, called her parents, then sobbed into her pillow all night. She was particularly prickly the next day in work.

After a few hours, her boss, fed up with the sulking, called her in.

"Mia, what you have to realise is, I want people on my team who are more concerned with finding the right idea than the right idea being theirs," she explained. "We value people who are focused on us winning as a company, as opposed to them winning, by being on the team. We're after people who are happy to hear when their idea doesn't work, because they know that will get us closer to the answer. People who don't cry or sulk when they get feedback because they don't see it as a judgement on them but instead a way of learning and improving."

Then she said, "Mia, when you heard you weren't on the team, you raged, sulked, thought it outrageous and unfair. You could have come and offered us your support with the project even though you didn't get in, letting us know that you were there for us if anything came up. You could have wondered why you weren't chosen, and when the time was right, asked for some feedback so you could learn for next time. Instead you made it about your ego, and as long as you do that, you won't be on any winning team."

Once she got over the shock of hearing this, Mia began to wonder whether always trying to be right in the past had stopped her from growing in deeper ways. She was super successful from the outside, but she felt fragile and insecure on the inside – always scared of failing in some way or getting something wrong. She was constantly worried about what others thought about her and, if someone was off with her, it could ruin her day. Mia was beginning to realise that her need to be right and her fear of getting things wrong was limiting her in many ways, but most importantly, affecting how she felt inside. As she progressed through the Ivy House Master Programme, she found the Courageous Learner skill particularly helpful. She began to see a different way of being: still super successful, but with much greater self-worth and a far greater desire to learn, grow and be a team player.

The five habits of Courageous Learners

Living above the line is the mindset of a Courageous Learner. Yes, they will slip below the line, sometimes several times a day. But, almost immediately they will be able to see what's happened, call it out, and do everything they can to bounce back.

Over the years, we've helped Courageous Learners develop a set of habits that make it easier for them to stay open, curious and above the line. Here are the five that make the biggest difference.

1. Courageous Learners have the courage to look at the raw facts

Courageous Learners have the courage to look at the raw facts of a situation or the behaviour of a person – including their own. When trying to understand something or someone, they go out of their way to collect as much information and data as possible, listen to different opinions and consider the merits of multiple arguments. They are fully aware that their lens on the world is not 'clean' and they try to look past their own beliefs, values and ambitions.

I was running one of the Ivy House Masterclasses once and was about to do a feedback exercise. All the delegates were working in groups and each member of the group was expected to give every other member individual feedback on their behaviour. Just before we started, I could see one of the delegates, Amy, welling up. Assuming she had a fear of upsetting others, I went over to reassure her that if her intent was good, it would all be fine. But I was wrong. Her tears were due to her fear of hearing stuff about herself that she didn't want to hear. She was worried that "other people would upset her". On talking more, it was clear that Amy believed that if people didn't like things about her or suggested she could do something better, it meant that she was 'worth' less.

Courageous Learners are able to hear other opinions about their behaviour because they know their self-worth isn't up for grabs. They know that if others experience them as 'too quiet' or 'too loud', this is just useful data that they can choose to action or not. They know that if someone finds a report they've written uninspiring, it's useful data, just as it is when they're told they write like a genius. Courageous Learners know that we're all a work in progress and are eager for feedback that can help inform their decisions.

2. Courageous Learners self-coach rather than self-judge

What do you do when you get something wrong? Does it depend how serious you think it is, and whether anyone saw you? Let's raise the stakes. Imagine you have to present in front of the whole company, including the CEO. You prep for weeks, but for whatever reason, your presentation just isn't great. The big day arrives, you can see people whispering at the back of the room and fidgeting at the front, and as you step forward, you get an ever-growing sinking feeling in the pit of your stomach. Finally, presentation over, you leave the stage.

What do you do now?

Do you take the opportunity, while your presentation is fresh in people's minds, to ask for feedback? Do you let them know that you're keen to improve, so would really appreciate them being totally honest with you? And then, when you've gathered the feedback, do you decide on your actions and move on, letting any feelings of embarrassment and frustration just pass straight through you?

Or…

Do you rush into the bathroom and hide with your head in your hands, wondering if you'll ever be able to show your face again?

When you do finally emerge, do you either avoid engaging in any conversation, or tell people constantly you know it was bad, without actually asking for any feedback? Do you spend weeks agonising over your 'failure', wondering how it has affected your prospects, having many sleepless nights and tense arguments with people around you in the process?

Many of us will empathise with the latter reaction, the first sounding just too good to be true. But you're vastly underestimating yourself if you believe you could never react in that balanced, open, positive way. With a little practice, you can. Don't fall back into the trap of thinking events dictate your behaviour – you can always choose. The ultimate question to ask yourself is: what sort of life (and world) do I want? One that's above or below the line?

Courageous Learners coach themselves without wasting any time on self-judgement. They know that beating themselves up makes them far more likely to fail than succeed and will also make them pretty unhappy along the way. They also know that, if they let themselves fall into a thought spiral, they're sending a message to their brain that they're under threat. What happens when we are under threat? We get defensive, we stop listening, we certainly stop learning and we do everything in our power to win. In other words, we fall below the line, and the results we get take a nose-dive too.

> **PAUSE AND REFLECT**
> ## Becoming your own coach
>
> Where have you spent most of your time to date? Self-coach or self-judge?
>
> Do you, like lots of people, believe that you're a good person because you beat yourself up when you get things wrong?
>
> Or do you see the value in being a self-coach and letting go of judging thoughts?
>
> What would it take for you to let go of your self-judge habit and begin to positively self-coach?

3. Courageous Learners hold their opinions lightly

Remember when we were talking about beliefs in Core Strength, and I asked you whether you thought your beliefs would be different if you'd grown up in a completely different family, in a different country with completely different political and religious views? Well opinions are the same. They're not truths, just ideas formed by the data we've collected throughout our lives so far.

When we hold on tight to our opinions, we're stopping any new data from going in. We're consciously closing ourselves down, digging a deep trench below the line, protecting our status quo and defending our ego.

But when we hold our opinions lightly, we free ourselves up to actually listen to others. We ask genuine questions and share everything we know in turn, so together we can deepen our knowledge and understanding of any given situation. And from that place – firmly above the line – we can make a decision. It may match our original opinion, or it may be different. Because Courageous Learners know that if they can't change their mind, they can't change anything.

Shona's company was merging two functions, and she was sure she'd come up with the right way to do it. She just needed to get her team to think that they'd come up with the idea, and they'd be good to go. She gave them advance notice of the meeting and told them that by the end of it they would need a decision, so they should all brainstorm ideas to bring with them.

On the day, she opened the meeting – which I'd been invited along to – telling them how much she valued their input and asked them one by one to share their ideas. As they went around the room explaining their thinking, she managed to find a way to show why each idea wouldn't work. By the time it got to the last person, Tom, the energy was so flat in the room I could see how hard it was for him to share what he'd come up with. When, at the end of the meeting, Shona unveiled her idea, the whole team simply agreed with her in a deflated manner and filed out of the room.

Shona achieved two things that day. First, she demotivated her team to such an extent that most of them left within six months. Second, she missed hearing some vital information that her team had uncovered during the research; information that, if she had heard it, would have prevented her losing her job ten months later.

Let's be clear. When I talk about holding your opinion lightly, I don't mean that it isn't okay to have strong opinions. Shona had a strong opinion about what needed to happen, based on a lot of thought and research, and that was great. She should absolutely have gone into that meeting and shared her strong opinion. But then, crucially, she should have said, "Tell me, what have I missed? What other ideas are there? Why is my idea good? Why is it bad? What could go wrong?" And once she'd asked the questions, she should have got curious and listened, really listened, to the answers. She should have helped her team pull apart her own idea, reject or refine it, and be truly creative in finding the best solution – together.

4. Courageous Learners fail forward and fail fast

In his book *Black Box Thinking*,[11] Matthew Syed opens with a startling statistic. In 2013, out of 3 billion airline passengers across the globe, 210 died in air accidents. He compares this with 400,000 *preventable* deaths in the US healthcare system alone. That's the equivalent of two jumbo jets full of passengers being killed by PREVENTABLE accidents in the US healthcare system EVERY DAY. So why do the two industries have such shockingly different safety records?

The reason is that the airline industry has an inbuilt culture of learning. Every single time there is an accident, the black box is recovered and analysed until every ounce of learning has been taken from the situation. The medical industry, on the other hand, is dogged by a culture of ego. It's created nurses who believe they can't question a surgeon's decision, even when they're concerned it could harm or, in some cases, kill the patient. This has led to repeated mistakes being made with misdiagnosed diseases because results aren't tracked, and data isn't shared. For some reason, it's become more important to keep senior medical staff's ego intact than to learn from mistakes. It's shocking and frightening in equal measure and the very definition of below-the-line thinking.

Courageous Learners know that if they're going to lead an extraordinary life, they need to develop certain skills. And they know that the only way to do that is to have a go, get it wrong, figure out why, make changes and do it again. Every day, fear of failure and the terror of 'losing face' get in the way of people becoming the best they can be. That's unutterably sad, and it's why Courageous Learners define a FAIL as nothing more than a First Attempt In Learning. Then they go out and do it, again and again.

PAUSE AND REFLECT

How courageous are you?

What would you like to be better at? Meeting new people? Dancing? Writing? Building your reputation? Having effective conversations? Being heard? Getting noticed?

And what's stopping you doing that?

Where are you on the Ownership Ladder?

Are you making excuses? Hoping things will change without you taking action?

Are you scared of asking for help?

Are you scared of failing or looking stupid?

Is it time to remember that you were born curious, you were born courageous, you were born to learn and grow?

5. Courageous Learners focus on changing themselves, not others

Who would you like to change? Your partner? Your mum or dad? Your teacher or boss?

Choose one. One person whose behaviour you would love to magically transform. Now grab a pen and paper and write down *everything* you would like to be different about them. Go to town.

Now, take a good look at your list… then crumple it up and throw it in the bin. Because Courageous Learners know that the only person they can change is themselves. Yes, we can ask others to change, but we can't make them change – just as no one can force us to change. Only we, as individuals and masters of our own destiny, have that power.

Jon and Lisa had been living together a while. Jon seemed relatively happy – he was busy in a job he enjoyed, loved playing rugby whenever he could and watched football with his mates most weekends. The only thing that got Jon down was Lisa. She was always on his case about doing more together with her and their joint friends and sharing more of the work around the house. That got on his nerves a bit, but he just organised to see his mates more, got home a bit later and tried to ignore her moaning. Obviously, this made things worse, and Lisa was getting more and more unhappy. When I asked what needed to change from her perspective, she responded with a long list of what she wanted Jon to do differently in turn.

Now fish your list out of the bin and imagine someone close to you had written a list like this about you. What would be on it? Be honest, even if it feels painful. Imagine this person begging, pleading with you to change your behaviour to make them happy. However much they implore you to change, however much pressure they put you under, can you see that unless YOU choose to change, the pleading will be pointless?

When Lisa and I spoke, I asked her what behaviour she was putting into her relationship with Jon. It included sending him emails at work to remind him to do things, leaving him lists at the weekend, texting him while he was out with his mates, and getting angry when, once again, he'd forgotten a date night. I asked what kind of results she thought her behaviour was getting? And whether she was prepared to try something different?

The following weekend, Lisa organised a weekend for herself that she would enjoy. She also asked Jon to let her know when, in the next few weeks, he would be around to discuss what they both wanted from the relationship. She told him she was keen to see if they wanted the same thing and, in preparation, she would have a think about what she wanted. She asked him if he would mind doing the same thing. She then got on with her weekend and had a great time. She spent some time really thinking about what was important to her and felt calm and open when she sat down with Jon a few days later.

What followed was the first effective conversation Jon and Lisa had had in ages. They both listened to each other, understood what each of them wanted and considered if they wanted enough of the same things. By changing how she was behaving towards Jon, Lisa had changed how she was feeling about herself, not to mention the quality of the conversation between herself and Jon.

When we give up trying to change others and put all our effort into thinking about how we want to behave, we restore ourselves to full power. We put our energy into what we can control, not what we can't... and in doing so inevitably create the change we longed for all along.

The gift of confidence

Of all the life-changing benefits of becoming a Courageous Learner, I believe the standout benefit is the gift of self-confidence. And that's amazing, because I have to tell you that, in over 20 years of coaching, I've found that so many people yearn for self-confidence. In a minute, I'll share how to satisfy that yearning. But for now, let's define what self-confidence actually is.

If confidence is the thought or feeling that you can rely on something or someone, then self-confidence is the thought or feeling that you can rely on yourself. If you have self-confidence, you trust your own abilities and judgements, and know that you will be okay no matter what.

There are two types of self-confidence: core confidence and situational confidence.

Core confidence

I pretty much always have core confidence. In other words, I have the deep-rooted feeling that no matter what happens around me, my wellbeing (my inner feeling of being well) will not be affected. I have this because I know two key things.

First, I know that every single feeling I have comes from a thought, which means that, if I have a feeling I don't like, I can just let the thought that is causing my discomfort pass through me. When I show up at an event with hundreds of strangers, yes, I may well get a thought which goes something like this: "OMG, I hate this! Who am I going to talk to? I'm so tired; I want to be home watching Netflix." But instead of grabbing on to it, I just let it go on its journey – and minutes later I'm focusing on the thought, "Wow, I'm so lucky to be here with all these incredible people. I am interested to hear the talks. This is exciting, I'm going to learn so much." So, in the first instance, my core confidence comes from knowing that, because I'm a human being, random thoughts of all kinds will pop into my head, but I have a choice as to which ones I want to hang out with.

Second, I know that my wellbeing, my feeling of self-worth, is *never* up for grabs. The problem with so many people living outside-in – believing that how they feel is dependent on what's going on around them – is that they're literally putting their self-worth in the hands of strangers. Why would you do that? Let me give you an example of how it plays out for me. I do a lot of writing – books, articles, speeches, masterclasses – and I work with a brilliant team of people whose opinions I trust. I put every piece of work I do in front of them for feedback, and they don't hesitate. "This doesn't work, it needs to flow better, you need to cut this out" – I've heard it all. If every time I got that kind of feedback I went into meltdown, my feeling of wellbeing would be all over the place. But here's the thing. I am not my work; I am not my results. My feelings of self-worth and wellbeing are inside me, fully intact all the time; they're not dependent on my annual earnings, the house I live in or how my hair looks on any particular day. I can hear their feedback and know it has nothing to do with me – just the piece of work I'm currently focused on. The only question is how *connected* I am to those inner feelings of confidence, wellbeing and self-worth (and we'll find out how to do that when we look at Proactive Wellbeing).

Interestingly, some people find my core confidence a bit threatening. You may even be reading this thinking that I sound a bit arrogant because I'm honest about pretty much always having access to my core confidence. But confidence isn't arrogance. I'm also acutely aware of what I'm really bad at, and I'm not afraid to call it out (and try to do something about it, if I can). The problem is – particularly in the UK, where I grew up – we come from a culture that encourages habitual self-deprecation and self-judgement, especially with regards to women. I refuse to buy into that culture, and I hope you won't either. It's part of what has landed us in our current environmental and social mess. You don't need to buy, beg or steal your sense of wellbeing. It's already within you, right now, just waiting for you to set it free.

Situational confidence

Inevitably, however, our confidence goes up and down depending on the situation we find ourselves in. Put me on stage with the brief to talk to a thousand people about living an extraordinary life, and I will feel situationally confident. Put me in a courtroom, with a wig on my head, to argue the case for a potential burglar – or in a gym, with the instruction that I must knock out two dozen reps – and I would not be confident. The reason for that is I don't have the relevant skills for either of those tasks. I've not worked on that craft.

Hone your craft

I can't tell you how many times people complain to me that they lack confidence in something, but when I ask them how much time they've spent trying to get good at it, they admit – very little. Here's a really basic truth – if you want to be good at something, you need to practise. You need to acquire the necessary knowledge, develop the skill (ideally from an expert) and then practise. I'm not saying that you can get good at everything. There's such a thing as talent, and I will never be a professional ballet dancer. But could I get better at ballet if I put in the hours? Yes, of course I could.

Situational confidence is not with us all the time – it's context-specific. I trust my ability to deliver a speech in front of a large crowd of people because I take being good at it very seriously. I've trained at drama schools and worked with expert speech writers, I prep my speeches weeks in advance and, before I deliver them, I practise them so often I'm generally able to do the whole thing without notes. The same applies to anything that's important to me. I want to cook healthy, tasty meals for my family, so I read books on how to do that and try the recipes out. When a recipe goes wrong, I don't throw all my pans in the bin and declare myself a failure – I learn from it and keep cooking.

But how does this work in more personal situations? For example, what if you want to be more confident with strangers, in bed with a lover, or about how you look? What then?

Simmy had a whole story about being born a shy person. She carried it around with her and regularly used it as an excuse to avoid anywhere she might have to meet new people, not to speak up in meetings and to generally hold herself back from life. Through being on the programme she realised that her apparent shyness was just the result of habitually hanging out with a certain set of thoughts which drove a certain set of behaviours: 'shy' ones. She had already started the process of creating some new habits, when she came to me at the end of a masterclass one day and said, "I get it. I get that I need to stop holding on to my unhealthy thoughts, but that still doesn't help me know what to do when I walk into a room full of strangers!" And she was right.

But here's the thing. This is the easy bit. There is a wealth of knowledge on pretty much everything out there, from books to podcasts to TED Talks to YouTube videos – the internet really is a Courageous Learners' bonanza, and most of it is free. You can access expertise on how to be better in bed, how to be vulnerable in a relationship, how to have a really difficult conversation. All you need to do then is practise, fail fast, adapt and practise some more. And here's the interesting thing: most people are okay with acquiring knowledge, but find the practising bit, especially when it has to happen in front of other people, incredibly hard. And I get it. It's a product of faulty thinking, the sort that attaches our self-worth to our performance. But when we're in the grip of that below-the-line thinking, we're motivated by being right and by winning, not by learning. And that, of course, brings us right back to where we were at the start of this chapter: stuck.

But the fascinating truth about confidence is that it's there, inside you, just waiting to shine. And all you have to do is check in whenever you feel scared or insecure and ask: what thoughts am I hanging out with? Am I above the line? If not, what can I do to get myself there? Do I have to let go of a thought, or seek out some raw facts, or hone my craft? There's *always* something you can do to get back to the position of power and wellbeing you were born with. That's the secret Courageous Learners never forget.

RECAP
Courageous Learner

- At any given moment, our behaviour is either below the line (driven by the need to be right, win and protect our ego) or above the line (motivated by a thirst for learning). Courageous Learners aren't perfect, but they do always know the standpoint from which they're operating. And when they fall below the line, they take ownership for getting back on track.

- Courageous Learners have the courage to look at the raw facts, gathering as much data as possible about a situation

---

or person or even themselves, and acknowledging that the lens of their beliefs and values might be limiting their vision.

- They also self-coach without self-judging, encouraging themselves to notice their behaviour and change what isn't working without falling into despair or defensiveness.

- Courageous Learners hold their opinions lightly, remaining open to other perspectives and ideas, and are willing to change their minds.

- They fail forward and fail fast, because they know it's the only way to improve, and because they understand that making mistakes doesn't diminish their self-worth.

- They acknowledge that the only person they can change is themselves, and that once they focus on doing that, their relationships and situations do indeed begin to shift.

- Courageous Learners have unshakeable core confidence, because their self-worth is not tied to how well they perform; and where they would like better situational confidence, they go out and find the relevant expertise, and put in the time to hone their craft.

Intentional Relationships

"Different people like different things."
Chris Rock

The Harvard Study of Adult Development is one of the longest-running studies on happiness in the world. Since launching in 1938, the project has followed 724 men from their teenage years through to old age (around 60 men, now in their 90s, are still left). The men come from diverse economic and social backgrounds, from Boston's poorest neighbourhoods to Harvard undergraduates, and over the decades, researchers have collected detailed health data on each of them, as well as asking the participants and their families questions about their lives and their mental and emotional wellness every two years.

What have they found?

That when it comes to leading an extraordinary life, relationships are *essential*.

"The surprising finding is that our relationships and how happy we are in our relationships has a powerful influence on our health," said Professor Robert Waldinger, the director of the study. "Taking care of your body is important but tending to your relationships is a form of self-care too. That, I think, is the revelation." The research found that close relationships, more than money or fame, are what keep us well. Social ties – whether between partners, neighbours, family members, friends or colleagues – protect us from life's discontents, help to delay mental and physical decline, and are better predictors of long and happy lives than social class, IQ or even genes.[12]

But we don't need science to inform us of the power of relationships. We've all been there – we might be in the perfect place, doing something we love... but if we argue with whomever we're with, it has a massive impact on how we feel that day. Alternatively, even if the world is throwing difficult event after difficult event at us – a conversation with an amazing friend or supportive community can make everything seem okay.

No, the real surprise, given the huge impact of relationships on our levels of happiness, is the fact that we're barely ever taught how to communicate effectively within our relationships. I've spent years coaching super-smart, successful leaders who often have disastrous relationships with their direct reports, partners or children. I've worked with married couples locked in vicious battles and families that, while they claim they love each other, don't treat each other with even a modicum of love. And I've seen at first hand, through our work with students on the Ivy House Award, how early these dysfunctional patterns start – often with friendships in school. 'Friends' who talk behind each other's backs, 'friends' who are friendly one day and cold the next, 'friends' who don't know the difference between making a joke and taking things too far, 'friends' who don't share what's going on for them but expect to be understood and loved. And the big one: 'friends' who would rather walk away than have an honest conversation about what isn't working.

Surely there's a better way?

Intentional Relationships – what does it mean?

Intentional Relationships is all about improving the quality of our relationships. Relationships of all kinds – intimate relationships, friendships, work-based relationships, as well as building an extended network. It's the skill of creating relationships from a place of trust, respect and understanding; it's about creating and maintaining these connections.

Why is it so important?

We've already seen ample evidence as to why we, as individuals, might want to get better at relationships. But it's also important for the wider world. With extremism on the rise, isolation in the UK dubbed an 'epidemic',[13] and social media entrenching social divisions, it isn't hard to see how our personal struggles are being reflected on a much bigger stage. If we want stronger businesses, healthier politics and fairer societies, we all have to take responsibility for leading the way towards more trusting, loving, thoughtful, joyful and productive relationships.

Learning to be good

Let's start by looking at what a relationship is. A relationship is what happens when two individuals put behaviour into the space between them.

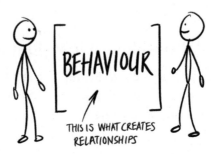

As you already know, we only know other people through their behaviour. If they're kind, we see them as kind. If they choose selfish or rude behaviour, we see them as selfish or rude. If that sounds incredibly simple, it's because it is. Relationships are like cakes: the sort of ingredients you put in determines the sort of cake you make. Putting in fun? It'll be fun. Putting in a lot of sniping and nagging? Not so much so.

PAUSE AND REFLECT

What behaviours do you put in?

Take a moment and think about a close relationship you are in that is not going so well at the moment.

What behaviours are you both putting in?

Be really honest. What would they say you were putting in?

What results are you getting by using those patterns of behaviour?

If you changed some of your behaviours, what impact would that have?

Once again, it's good news: you have a choice.

YOU ALWAYS
GET TO CHOOSE THIS

EVENT + BEHAVIOUR
= RESULT

No matter what the 'event' in your relationship – an affair, a harsh word, a cold shoulder, a misunderstanding – we always get to choose our response to that event. What's more, every time we choose our response, we get to impact the overall nature of the relationship. We move it further in one direction or another. That's not to say you can't choose to be unkind if someone is unkind to you or angry if they've betrayed you. The important thing is to realise that's a choice. It might sound harsh, but the fact is:

- No one forced you to slam the door – you chose that.

- No one ignored you so much you had to sleep with someone else – you chose that.

- No one made you ignore the issues in the relationship for so long you struggled to see the way back – you chose that.

- No one gave you so much work that you couldn't help but feel overwhelmed – you chose that.

- No one made you so tired and stressed you couldn't be a good friend – you chose that.

This can feel challenging, but it's also liberating. If we want to get good at relationships, first we need to take 100% Ownership for the behaviour we bring to them, and the care we take to maintain them. When we do that, the one skill most likely to determine your future happiness becomes as easy as ABC.

The ABC of relationships

ASPIRATION &
AGREEMENTS

BELIEFS &
BEHAVIOURS

COMMUNICATION &
CONVERSATIONS

Pick a relationship that really matters to you and isn't going so well at the moment. Use the review below to examine it and understand more clearly what's going on. As always, I am going to ask you to be courageously honest as I go through each element of the review. Try to stay above the line.

(Note: a number of the questions below relate to intimate relationships. If you are reviewing a friendship, family, work or school relationship, just adapt the questions to fit.)

ASPIRATIONS

It's just as important to have a clear, shared, articulated vision for your relationship as it is for your life. This isn't just about where and how you want to live (if you're reviewing a partnership), but how you'll treat each other, deal with conflict, communicate, raise children and spend your money. It must include a deep understanding of each other's personal visions and values as well as a detailed vision for what you're both aspiring to in the relationship.

In work relationships, having an agreed vision for what 'good' looks like is equally important. What's your boss's preferred method of communication? How frequently would they like contact with you? Are you able to discuss a wide variety of topics? What matters to them? How can you help them achieve their goals and how can they reciprocate? When you think about it, it's astonishing how rarely we have these kinds of conversations in our professional lives – and how much stress and misunderstanding could be spared if we did.

Ask yourself:

Do you have a clear, agreed and articulated vision for your relationship (ideally written down)?

Does it take account of your personal visions as well as the vision for the relationship?

Does it go into enough detail?

Have you both agreed what 'good' looks like for you both?

Review:

Give yourself a score out of ten in terms of how 'sorted' this element of your relationship is and make a note of any actions you'd like to take.

> "I did the review on my relationship with my boss. I was becoming increasingly concerned that she was regretting hiring me. After the review I went and talked it through with her and asked her what 'good' looked like for her. At first she looked at me like I'd gone mad and then said, 'I'm fed up with having to drag information out of you. I never know how you're doing on any project and it makes me feel really worried. I don't want to be caught off guard by my boss if a project runs over. You stress me out.'

"In that moment I realised that I had assumed she liked to work like I did: only hearing about things when there was an issue, or once they were completed. I'd thought I'd been doing a great job by keeping it all from her, when she wanted the exact opposite. The minute I knew that, we had a really good conversation about how she wanted me to keep her informed differently. The mad thing about it all is that the conversation took 15 minutes and I'd been stressing about our relationship for over a year!"

Ollie, 32, retail buyer

AGREEMENTS

Successful relationships are based on clear, articulated and shared agreements. Unfortunately, most of our relationships are based on unspoken expectations instead. These expectations operate like invisible rules, rules that we judge each other by and get angry or upset about when they're unknowingly broken. So, once you've defined a shared vision for your relationship, it's important to make clear agreements that you'll both stick to as you turn your vision into a reality. They can cover any part of your relationship, including money, communication, trust, support, roles, independence, friendships, family, change, respect and responsibilities.

They look something like this:

- I agree to always let you know if I'm unhappy with something in our relationship.
- I will always make time to discuss any issues we have within a day or two of them being raised.
- I will not engage romantically with anyone else while in a relationship with you.

Or for work relationships:

- I will meet my deadlines and let you know in advance if anything will get in the way of that.
- I will report any threats to the success of the project as soon as I hear of them.
- I will manage my own energy and emotional state so I can show up positively to our relationship.

"Historically my mum and I had got on brilliantly, but when I went to university and came home in the holidays it seemed we did nothing but argue. Finally, beside myself with the exhaustion of it all, I sat down and showed her the ABC of relationships. We had a brilliant conversation about what we wanted for our relationship as I matured into adulthood, but the really interesting thing was the chat we had on expectations and agreements. Being in university, I was used to running my own life and doing my own thing, when and how I choose to. It was my 'expectation' that I could do exactly the same when I came home. Mum's expectations, however, were very different. She expected me to tell her where I was going, when I would be back and to adhere to some house rules.

"What we both realised was that we'd never shared these expectations with each other, much less agreed on them. We spent a decent amount of time considering what a good solution would look like for both of us. She recognised my new-found, and much cherished, independence; I recognised her need to know I was safe and her desire that I contribute to family life. I have to say it was one of the best conversations we've ever had and has set us up for many more."

Chloe, 20, studying fashion

Ask yourself:

Have you ever had a conversation around the agreements that would support your vision?

Do either of you often have the feeling of letting the other down without quite knowing why?

Does one of you often end up disappointed, angry or frustrated?

Do you have a clear and agreed set of agreements in place (ideally written down)?

Review:

Give yourself a score out of ten in terms of how 'sorted' this element of your relationship is and make a note of any actions you'd like to take.

BELIEFS

Remember, beliefs are thoughts we have bought into to such an extent that we see them as truths. Our beliefs create the lens we see the world through.

The problem is we often forget we're actually wearing our belief glasses, which leads us to assume that what we think is right – and that if someone disagrees with us, they're wrong. Limiting beliefs can be a secret poison in a relationship if they go unchecked. In the context of relationships, there are four types of beliefs we need to be particularly mindful of:

1. Beliefs you have about relationships in general, such as, "most relationships fail in the end", "you have to work at a relationship to make it a success" or "you can never be 100% honest with another person".

2. Beliefs you have about the relationship itself, such as, "we don't want the same things", "I can't be happy without him", or "our earnings will never be equal and that will cause issues".

3. Beliefs you have about the other person, such as, "she will never change", "she's too good for me" or "he never listens".

4. Beliefs you have about yourself in the relationship, such as, "I can't be myself in this relationship", "he brings out the worst in me" or "she makes me a better person".

"I hated doing this exercise, really hated it. When I realised that I really believed George was better than me, and that it had been driving my needy and clingy behaviour, I was embarrassed and frightened all at the same time. He was never going to stay with me if I continued to be like that, and because of my belief that I would never find anyone else that good (because he was so much better than me), I was scared.

"It took me months to finally realise that my belief was just a thought I had bought into and I could let it go. When I did finally let it go, it made space for me to really enjoy being with George without always worrying he would rather be with someone else – but more importantly I was also able to focus my energy on fully becoming me. Getting to know me, what I loved, how I wanted to spend MY time, what mattered to me. And realising that if George wanted to be with that person then great; but, if he didn't, that would be okay too. I would survive."

Denny, 43, architect

Ask yourself:

What limiting beliefs are you holding on to about relationships in general, a specific relationship, the other person and yourself?

What limiting beliefs do you believe *they* are holding on to?

How prepared do you think both of you are to let go of these limiting beliefs?

Have you let go of *all* limiting beliefs regarding this relationship?

Review:

Give yourself a score out of ten in terms of how 'sorted' this element of your relationship is and make a note of any actions you would like to take.

BEHAVIOURS

Let's say it yet again: relationships are created through behaviours. Push yourself to think about the behaviours you put 'in' to the relationship on a daily basis, and how proactive you are at working 'on' the relationship. Generally, this is an area in which people go very easy on themselves, so to keep yourself honest, try considering what the other person would say about you.

"Thinking about what my dad would say, rather than me, put a very different spin on this. I would have said that my behaviour was fine. I was polite, answered his questions, rang him once a week and checked how he was doing. But when I thought about it from his perspective, it was completely different. He would have said I did the bare minimum to keep the relationship alive. I never shared anything with him about what was going on in my life and therefore he didn't feel trusted by me or close to me. Similarly, although I asked him about his job, I never enquired about his relationship with my step-mum, his hopes, his dreams, his worries or his concerns. I was like the cardboard cutout version of a grown-up son.

"Thinking about my behaviours got me to reconsider what kind of relationship I actually wanted with him. Did I want this surface, perfunctory one or something closer and more meaningful? I knew he did but what did I want? And, if I wanted more, was I prepared to put in the behaviour to make it happen? I decided I did. I've since been working on dropping the really unhelpful and unkind beliefs I've been carrying around with me for years and changing the behaviour I put into the relationship. The change has been almost instantaneous."

Al, 22, nurse

Ask yourself:

Looking at your daily behaviours, what percentage would you say are nurturing to the relationship and which are not? Note: They're either nurturing or not, neutral is not nurturing.

Have you both made it easy for the other to get to know you?

Are you trustworthy in the relationship?

Do you believe them to be?

Are you both supportive, respectful, kind and loyal?

Are you both proactive, making time to work on the relationship and changing if necessary?

Are you as interested in each other's goals as much as your own?

How much ownership do you take for your behaviour – when you get it wrong do you apologise and change?

Do they?

Review:
Give yourself a score out of ten in terms of how 'sorted' this element of your relationship is and make a note of any actions you would like to take.

COMMUNICATION

There are so many different ways to communicate. Verbal communication is just one. Think about the energy you bring to your relationship, the body language, the quality of your listening, the tone of your words and how often you're affectionate (if appropriate). Some people have a habit of saying all the right things, but everything else they do tells a different story.

> "I've realised that my wife mainly communicates nonverbally. She huffs and puffs, rolls her eyes, says everything is 'fine' through tight lips, when it's clearly not. If I've done something she doesn't like, she doesn't tell me but can sulk for days. I used to spend ages dragging it out of her but in the past few years I've stopped. I just let her quietly fume

and move to a different room. I think I've given up. The problem is it makes for an awful atmosphere in the house. We hardly ever eat together as a family now. The kids are pretty much monosyllabic with us both. I think I thought that by ignoring it, I was avoiding conflict and that was a good thing. But now I realise that was just an excuse because I didn't really know how to handle it. I was scared it would tip her over the edge and she'd storm out. I'm going home to have the conversation. We have a lot of work to do."

Martin, 53, doctor

Ask yourself:

What energy do you bring to the relationship?

What energy do they bring?

How positive is your communication (other than in words), i.e. do you get moody, roll your eyes, use silence, withdraw, get angry, disagree, display vulnerability or avoid honesty?

How positive is their communication, outside of conversations?

How would you score the way you both communicate within the relationship?

Review:

Give yourself a score out of ten in terms of how 'sorted' this element of your relationship is and make a note of any actions you'd like to take.

CONVERSATIONS

Conversations are the glue that holds a relationship together, and their quality and frequency determine whether your glue is weak and flaky or watertight. Effective conversations can only happen when both people show up above the line, motivated by learning rather than being right.

> "Winning. That is all that really matters to both me and my boyfriend. Every time we try and discuss something other than normal everyday rubbish – and sometimes even then – we are just competing to be right. He pulls out the more intelligent card, using long words and quoting theories he learnt during his degree. I pull out the emotionally intelligent card, claiming he is basically a Neanderthal, and if that doesn't work, I get furious. Our arguments are exhausting. Literally exhausting. If I am honest, I am not really sure either of us knows how to show up motivated to learn, but we are going to have to try or we are going to die young!"

> Maddy, 23, trainee accountant

Ask yourself:

When issues do come up, do you talk openly about the conflicts and find resolutions together?

Are you both fully open to feedback from each other?

Do you make time for important conversations as issues arise?

Do you both enter into conversations with the intent of moving forward positively? (Or does one or both of you try to win the argument?)

Does one or both of you use extreme emotion to manipulate the discussion?

How would you score the quality and timeliness of your conversations?

Review:

Give yourself a score out of ten in terms of how 'sorted' this element of your relationship is and make a note of any actions you would like to take.

The ABC of relationships can be used at any time in a relationship and for any kind of relationship. Ideally it would be completed by both people independently and then discussed, but if this isn't possible (or it would just seem too weird), do it yourself to understand what may be going on. And then have an effective conversation to move the relationship forward (don't worry – we'll cover how to do that later in this chapter).

How do you show up to your relationships?

Hopefully by now, you'll have a much clearer idea of the state of the relationship you chose to review. You may have decided a conversation is needed – and that's great – but before you do that, I'd like to take a few more minutes of your time to ask you a few more questions.

Here are my top five relationship questions. You can ask them in relation to this specific relationship or be more general. Whatever you do, have the courage to look at the raw facts, try to stay motivated by learning, and see past your own limiting beliefs.

1. Are you a Giver or a Taker?

In his bestselling book *Give and Take*, Wharton professor of or-ganisational psychology Adam Grant asks the question: are you a Giver or a Taker? Givers are people who are genuinely interested in supporting others. They want to put good into their relation-ships and are not looking for a payback. They have an 'abundance' mentality – they believe that there is enough love and kindness in the world for everyone and they give it freely. Takers, on the other hand, have a scarcity mentality. They believe resources and opportunities are limited and, if they are to be happy in life, they have to fight for what they can get. They're almost always looking for what they can get out of a situation, to see how they can come off best and aren't really concerned about the outcome for others.

Grant did a whole load of research into whether Givers or Takers are more successful in life and, in the process, he discovered a third type. A Matcher. Matchers are the quid pro quo people, the ones who keep score. I took the bins out last time; you have to do it this time. I've had you around for dinner twice; you now need to invite me back. I complimented you yesterday; you now need to respond. Matchers keep tallies in their head. They give what they think is acceptable and 'right', no more or no less. They're motivated by playing by their rules and judge anyone who doesn't.

To get the hang of these different types, think about how you handle dishwashers. Yes, dishwashers. The Givers will open the dishwasher to put something in, see it's full and clean, and empty it. They don't need any praise or thanks – they just do it. The Takers, on the other hand, seeing that the dishwasher is clean and full, leave their dirty plate next to the dishwasher (assuming no one has seen them) and get out of the kitchen as soon as possible before they get 'caught'. The Matchers know exactly who did it last time and who's turn it is this time and get really annoyed if they're asked to do it when it isn't 'fair'.

While this may seem like a mundane example, these sorts of everyday dynamics can make or break relationships. And when it comes to bigger emotional stuff, the same behaviours play out.

Givers show care and interest in others' wellbeing. They'll go out of their way to support someone even when there's absolutely nothing in it for them. They notice people's energy and take note of people's emotional needs. They openly share what's going on for them as a mark of trust, and they care when someone else is hurting – not becoming the rescuer but acknowledging their pain.

Conversely, Takers put in just enough to get what they want out of the other person. It's not that they won't share stuff about themselves; they do, but usually to achieve the goal they've set themselves in the relationship. For example, they may be on top sparkly form with a potential employer – pulling out their most charming behaviour to ensure the new boss likes and rates them – but then put in the bare minimum with their family. Until they want something that is – attention, a favour – and then the charm comes out in full force. Takers often get fed up with other people's emotions but take their own very seriously. They often see Givers as weak, not understanding the rules of the jungle, but they'll happily use them to get stuff done and help them meet their goals. They find Matchers annoying because they'll often call them out on their taking, pointing out when their behaviour is 'unfair'.

Finally, Matchers keep scores in relationships. You tell me something about you? I'll do the same. You do something for me? I'll reciprocate. They do this because it's fair, and fairness is the guiding rule of a Matcher. But the problem is, 'fair' doesn't inspire love, connection, joy or caring. It can feel cold, calculating and disingenuous. Not the kind of people most of us want to be in a relationship with.

Because here's the interesting thing about this. Everyone wants to be in relationships with Givers, to employ Givers, to have them as friends. Takers want to hang out with Givers. Matchers want to hang out with Givers. Givers want to hang out with Givers. No wonder they're also the most successful people in life.

But here's the twist in the tale. If you're sitting there calculating whether it's worth it to make all that effort to become a Giver, that puts you squarely in the Taker and Matcher camps. True Givers don't give a stuff what their behaviour means to their bank balance or their career progression. They do it because it's who they want to be. They want to lovingly connect with other people. They want to support others. They want to bring good to the world. So be a Giver because it's who you want to be, otherwise don't bother.

Bella and her brother Matt weren't close. Bella was angry with Matt because during his teen years he had gone off the rails, and to Bella it had felt like he'd torn the family apart. He had seemingly absorbed most of his parents' emotional energy, caused endless arguments and endless pain. Now, eight years later, he'd really got his life together. He was married to the lovely Samira and had a baby, Amelia, who everyone adored. His relationship with his parents was repaired and better than it had ever been.

But Bella just couldn't forgive him. She was angry, really angry. She blamed Matt for what she saw as her ruined teenage years. Why should he now have a great relationship with her parents when he'd caused them so much pain? Why did they forgive him? It just wasn't fair. When Bella came to coaching, we went first to the Ownership Ladder and she recognised she was firmly stuck at 'Blaming Others'. But the big breakthrough came when Bella recognised this had nothing to do with Matt and everything to do with who she wanted to be. Bella was clearly behaving like a Matcher. She saw the situation as unjust and wanted Matt to suffer for the pain he'd caused. The question was – who did she want to be? Irrespective of Matt and her parents, what energy and behaviour did she want to bring to the world?

2. Are you a Drain or a Radiator?

As I've mentioned, in our household we have five teenage girls and what that means, apart from the need for endless lifts, is that we have a house full of their friends. Girlfriends, boyfriends, friends of friends and sometimes the odd random teenager that seemingly no one knows. But other than the expense of having to keep the fridge full, this gives me the opportunity to play one of my favourite games: "who would I employ?"

As they all lounge about, talking over each other, arguing about the music and what kind of pizza to order, I ask myself just that question. Knowing nothing about them except for how they interact, I decide who I would offer a job to, and those you couldn't pay me to employ. Who gets the nod? The Radiators, every time.

You know Radiators. When they show up, everyone lights up just that little bit more. They're the ones who ask after others, share a funny story and look on the bright side. They can be extroverts, filling the space with stories and laughter, or they can be introverts, deeply listening and bringing all their attention and warmth to a conversation. This isn't about being loud or quiet – it's about bringing a positive energy to the room.

You doubtless also know Drains. When they show up, it's as if a black hole has begun to suck the energy from the room. They come in many different varieties, too. There are the 'moany groany' types, who love to bitch and complain; the 'look at me' types, who demand so much attention it's exhausting just being near them; the 'you do all the work' types who neither share anything about themselves nor ask you any questions; and the 'walk on eggshells' types who are all charm and chumminess one minute, then give you the cold shoulder the next.

We all know Drains and Radiators. We can tell because, when we leave them, we are either energised or drained. The important question is, which one are you? Be really honest with yourself.

PAUSE AND REFLECT
What energy do you bring?

Imagine yourself as a fly on the wall, watching yourself with different groups of people.

What behaviour/energy do you put in?

Are you one way with work colleagues, another with your friends and another with your family? Who are you a Drain to, and who are you a Radiator to?

What impact does that have on others?

What impact do you want to have going forward?

---

3. What games are you playing?

When we've been in certain relationships for a while, it's all too easy to develop patterns of behaviour that turn those relationships into something like unhealthy games.

One of the relationship 'games' that's most common, and most useful to understand, is the drama triangle. This is a model developed by psychologist Dr Stephen Karpman to describe the three roles people often slip into in their relationships: victim, rescuer or persecutor.[14]

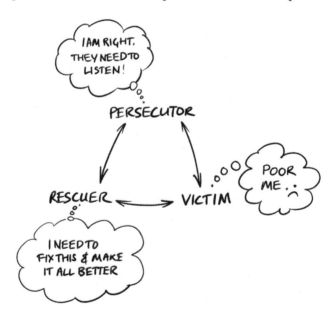

Victims

The starting point of a victim is "Poor me!" They see themselves as oppressed, powerless, dejected and ashamed, and often come across as 'super-sensitive', needing special treatment from others. They sit way down on the Ownership Ladder, taking little or no ownership for their situation and so claiming no power to sort it out.

When someone takes the position of victim, they're inviting someone to rescue them, making someone else out to be the persecutor – or both. For example, this is the person who gets themselves into a state of massive anxiety and, in the process (consciously or unconsciously), invites others to take the action they themselves are too overwhelmed to consider. When in the role of victim, people have real difficulty making decisions, solving problems, finding pleasure in life, or understanding how their own thinking and behaviour contributes to their struggle.

Rescuers

The starting point of the rescuer is "Let me help you!" They work hard to help and take care of others, and sometimes think they need to do this to feel good about themselves. A common trait of a natural rescuer is to spend so much time focusing on the needs of others that they neglect their own. Rescuers are often attracted to victims, who give them someone to help and therefore a way to feel good about themselves.

Rescuers are frequently hassled, overworked and tired... as well as often strangely resentful for all the help and support they freely give.

Persecutors

The starting point of the persecutor is "It's all your fault!" Persecutors criticise and blame the victim, and can be controlling, rigid, authoritative, angry and unpleasant. They keep the victim feeling oppressed through threats and bullying.

Persecutors are inflexible, don't show vulnerability and are often seen as callous. Persecutors fear being victims themselves. They can yell and criticise but often don't actually solve any problems or help anyone else solve the problem. They enjoy the fuss and don't really want it to end.

What I've described here are the most extreme versions of these three roles, but it's possible to spot people playing milder versions of them on a pretty regular basis. The important thing to recognise is that each role has a 'payoff' or benefit for the person playing it. When we play the victim, we ensure we don't have to take responsibility for our situation and get others to do that for us. When playing the role of rescuer, we get to feel good about helping people 'weaker' than ourselves, and often have an excuse for not addressing our own issues. And, when we are in persecutor mode, we feel a sense of (false) power by controlling and manipulating others.

Most of us have a natural preference for one of the roles but can quickly switch if we think a different one will be more advantageous to our situation. For example, you may be a natural rescuer, but whenever you get overwhelmed by everything you are doing for others, you may become a persecutor, blaming everyone around you for feeling so exhausted. In the same way, if your natural tendency is to be a victim, you too can jump to persecutor if calling for help isn't working, and you think yelling might get you what you want.

Alice's husband had left her. All of a sudden, she found herself living alone with her two teenage sons, Dylan and Gus. It wasn't the plan she'd had for her life and that made her very angry. While dealing with her pain over her failed marriage, which she termed an 'abandonment', she adopted the role of victim whenever she could. She expected her sons to 'look after her' as her husband had done and got very angry with them (jumping to the role of persecutor within seconds) when they wanted to get on with their life. She repeated endless tales of the hardship of being a 'single mother' – she was working AND looking after the kids. The more she did this, the more her boys jumped between the roles of rescuer and persecutor – first, trying to support their mum by showing sympathy, and then getting angry with her for not getting on with her life or taking any ownership for the situation she found herself in.

Almost everyone has encountered a drama triangle in their life. For many people it's a regular feature in their relationships and keeps them stuck in unhappy dynamics. The crucial question is, how do you get out of it?

As ever, the first step is to move to a place of awareness. Recognise what's going on. After that, you have to summon the courage to stop 'playing the game'.

For example, if you're usually a rescuer, when you're confronted with a victim you need to stop trying to solve the victim's problems and recognise that your behaviour is 'enabling' them to stay stuck. Even just adapting your language from "how can I help?" to "how can I be useful?" will allow you to offer support while placing the 'victim' squarely in control of their own situation.

If you default to victim behaviour, then learning to voice what you need and want – practising being vulnerable without expecting others to fix the situation for you – is key.

Persecutors must recognise that their feelings of empowerment stem from taking advantage of others' powerlessness. They need to find alternative ways to make themselves feel good and in control.

Recognising where you naturally go in the drama triangle, and using this awareness to break this repetitive pattern, is a powerful way to start transforming your relationships.

PAUSE AND REFLECT

What dramas are you engaged in?

Be courageously honest – where do you tend to go in the drama triangle?

Which relationships does it show up in?

How would that relationship be without that pattern?

What do you want to do about it?

4. Are you worthy of trust?

While relationships are created by the behaviour we put in, what underpins that behaviour is trust. Trust is the firm belief in the reliability, truth, or ability of someone or something. And what's tricky about it is that it often feels intangible. Someone may say all the right things, but we may still have a deep sense of mistrust. This will inevitably get in the way of the relationship.

In my experience, the best way to understand trust in any relationship is to look at it in terms of character and competence. You may well trust someone's character, i.e. trust they have good intent, yet not trust their ability to get the job done. Conversely, someone may be really good at their job, but you might fear that, despite getting excellent results, they'll stab you in the back.

For a moment bring to mind someone you don't trust, and answer these questions:

Character questions

Do you trust their motives?

Do you think they are motivated to do right by you or are just looking out for themselves?

Do you believe they will do what they say they will?

Do you trust that they're telling you the truth?

Do you think they say one thing to you and another to someone else?

Competency questions

Do you think they have the necessary skills to do what's needed of them?

Do they have the necessary knowledge?

Do they have the necessary experience?

What's their track record on things like this?

Have they had previous successes or failures in this area?

When we ask questions like these of others, it becomes easy to see where trust falls down – either their character, competence or both. But the really interesting work happens when we ask them of ourselves.

Think about yourself in the context of the relationship you reviewed earlier. Are you worthy of trust? Should the other person trust your character? Do you have good intent? Do you do what you say you will? Do you treat them with respect, care and loyalty? Are you honest with them? Should they trust your competence? Do you have the skills and knowledge to do what you say?

In my experience, people find it really easy to understand why they don't trust others – and far less easy to understand why others may not trust them. They tend to feel 'outraged' when people don't trust them and blame the other person for their lack of trust… as opposed to taking the time to really look deeply at themselves and see why that may be the case.

> "I knew my boyfriend loved me; that wasn't the issue. But I discovered that in certain areas he didn't trust me. He said I made lots of promises to change things but often didn't follow through. I would promise to find more time for us to be together and then not do it or forget. He said the impact of that was that he couldn't trust what I said. When he first said it, I got really angry and defensive – didn't he see all the things I did for him, for us? But then, when I calmed down, I realised he was right. I often didn't do what I said I would, and I suspected it was the same in work too. I finally got the courage to ask the people I worked with if this was also a problem for them and it turned out it was. I'm now completely determined to be more trustworthy going forward."
>
> Natalie, 29, coder

"After learning about trust, I did a trust survey with my team. What I learnt was that, while they trusted my intent, they didn't trust that I would follow through on my commitments. This made them wary of the agreements we made and resulted in them questioning whether their own efforts would be worthwhile. They also didn't trust my ability to hold others to account in the team, noticing how I often let underperformers stay in the team and not deal with them properly. Finally, they had big issues around my ability to run a meeting well. They felt we wasted lots of time and never got real clarity on direction. All of this was pretty hard to hear, but I'm grateful they had the courage to tell me. I now know exactly what I need to work on."

Helena, 38, computer games developer

Trust sits at the foundation of every relationship and it manifests itself through behaviour. The minute a manager says, "I really need to improve my meeting management skills and I'm going to do something about it," their trust scores will soar. Nobody needs you to be perfect in a relationship (good luck trying), but people do need to know that you can be trusted to do the right thing – and in times when you don't have the competence to do that, that you'll own up to it and do something about it.

Rebuilding trust

One of the most common things we hear people say when we talk about trust is: "Once my trust has been broken it can't be rebuilt." Well, like most things, that's just a belief. Trust can absolutely be rebuilt, and there are countless examples to prove it… but only when both parties are committed to the task.

For trust to be rebuilt, the area in which it has broken down needs to be clearly identified. Taking Helena's example above, she learnt that her team trusted her intent, but they didn't trust her integrity to follow through. They also didn't trust in her ability to manage poor performance or run meetings well. Thanks to her survey, Helena was clear what she needed to do to rebuild trust. So, having shared her findings with the team, she gave them permission to call her out on it if she didn't follow through, did some training on team effectiveness, and then asked her team to feed back again on the changes they saw.

In doing this, Helena wasn't only demonstrating the behaviours of a truly Courageous Learner. She was helping her team see her in a new light by asking them to support her as she learned and grew.

5. Team Cow or team Rhino?

This is our final question in this chapter, and it's a very simple one. I hope that through the past few pages you've been thinking a lot about the relationships in your life and specifically the ones that are not working as well as you'd like.

So, what you really need to ask yourself is: are you going to be a Rhino, acknowledge reality and do something about it? Or, are you going to hang out at the bottom of the Ownership Ladder – a Cow, continuing to make excuses and blame others for the state of your relationships?

The thing is, if you don't vote for team Rhino, the stories, models and examples I've already shared with you are irrelevant. If you want to create relationships that bring you long-term joy, health and growth, then you need to be intentional about them. And guess what? Yep, it's your choice.

Conversations – the big enabler

Knowing all these things about how relationships work puts you way ahead of most of the population. Unfortunately, having all this knowledge means nothing without the ability to have effective conversations.

Conversations in a relationship are like the oil in a car – without them the engine stops turning. We need them to keep our relationships honest, authentic and on track. They enable us to deal with issues before they get too big. They allow us to gather more data, so we can see things from different perspectives, get curious and listen before we make judgements. They allow us to say sorry, to get to know the other person at a deeper level, and to come together to solve a problem and move forward in a positive way. They are the fuel for relationships of any kind – with a loved one, a parent, a friend, a boss – and taking the time to get good at them will turbocharge every aspect of your life.

Think about someone you are in a relationship with that you've argued with recently. Pick a relationship that's different from the one you worked on before and recall your last few heated or difficult conversations.

Now, start off by asking: in the heat of the argument, were you above or below the line? Motivated by learning or winning? Were you busy trying to find out what was really going on for them or was it more important for you to be right?

Move on to your behaviours. Ask yourself: what kind of behaviour did you choose in the moment? Did you believe that it was them, or the situation, that was causing you to behave in that way? Did you go into the discussion prepared to change? And, if you agreed to change, did you do it willingly or through gritted teeth, because you just wanted the discussion to be over? Did you agree to something you have no intention of doing? Or will you honour your agreement whilst also resenting it?

Effective conversations only happen when people are above the line: when you have good intentions, when you want to learn and find a solution that works. So, be honest with yourself. Are you usually above or below the line in important conversations? How is that working out?

If part of your vision for an extraordinary life is to have successful, loving, respectful and fun relationships, then learning the art of conversation is going to be essential.

PAUSE AND REFLECT

Are conversations adding to or taking away from your life?

Think for a moment. What's the nature and quality of the conversations around your family dinner table?

Do you all show trust and respect by sharing what's going on for you?

Do you listen to each other without agenda? Or do you revert to banter – a lot of fun at times, but also used as a technique to avoid real conversation?

Is the conversation snipey, competitive or aggressive? Or is it polite and calm but devoid of any real curiousity or sharing?

Do the conversations you have leave you feeling loved, supported and energised, or do you feel drained and a bit empty?

Ultimately, conversations go well or badly because of two key factors. Let's call them out.

1. Intent

The 'real' intent that sits behind a conversation is the biggest reason they go wrong. Imagine the scenario: you've argued with your partner and you ask for a chat to sort it out. Unbeknown to you, they are below the line and their intent is "for you to see how wrong you are and for you to apologise" (i.e. to win). Just think for a moment. If they set out with that intent, how well do you think the conversation will go? Now, also imagine you have the same intent; that you also want to get them to see how wrong they've been and to force them to apologise. What are the chances of the conversation going well now?

To master the art of effective conversations, we need to drag our intent above the line. That means being motivated by learning and moving forward positively, as opposed to winning or being right. When we have good intent, we are:

- Transparent – sharing what's really going on for us, how we're truly thinking and feeling.

- Accountable – we're honest about our actions and our part in causing the issue.

- Curious – we deeply listen to the other person, including listening for things they may not be saying.

- Compassionate – we understand that people may not always say things in the best way, but that doesn't mean we should blow up or stop listening.

In my experience this is another area in which people find it hard to be honest with themselves. They tend to vehemently argue that they had good intent for a conversation that didn't go well, right up to the point when we ask them to look at the behaviour they chose.

"Doing this work was a shocker for me. I realise that my intent in pretty much every conversation I go into is to get my own way. I do it with my wife and kids and I do it with my team. I go in and tell them I want to discuss something that I've already made my mind up about. Then we play this charade where I pretend to listen to all their ideas and then tell them mine. The meetings always feel flat at the end and I think we all walk away thinking 'what a waste of time'. I've realised that I need to hold my opinions lightly and genuinely listen to what they have to say. I also need to be honest up front and say I have a view, then invite them to build on it as well as coming up with other ideas. I'm actually really embarrassed about this."

Pav, 44, CMO of a sports agency

"I'm known in my group of friends as being a really feisty person. Someone with strong opinions. But now I realise that, while I can have strong opinions, conversations aren't actually about winning and losing but about learning. I have a trick I use all the time – I play the intellectual card. When someone comes out with an argument I disagree with, I try to belittle them by pulling out some spurious bit of research and sounding more knowledgeable than them. The whole thing is designed to put me on top. I feel like a bit of an idiot. I've blocked listening to other people most of my life because I'm so busy trying to win. I suspect I've missed a lot and hurt quite a few people. I'm also a bit angry because in school we were taught that the 'toughest man wins' and admitting we had stuff to learn was a sign of weakness. How wrong could I have been?"

Henry, 35, banker

153

2. Behaviours

Your behaviour is the second biggest influence on whether a conversation goes well or badly. You may think your intent is good, but if your behaviour is defensive, aggressive and devoid of curiosity and caring, you'll repeat the same old pattern again and again.

Our behaviour in conversations tends to fall into three types: aggressive, avoidant, or effective.

Aggressive and avoidant behaviours are the hallmarks of someone below the line. They may seem like opposites, but they're both motivated by winning or being right. Interestingly, whilst many people below the line default to one or the other, some jump between the two at a moment's notice – one minute refusing to talk (avoidant) and the next yelling at the top of their voice (aggressive). It's a surprisingly common, and totally ineffective, mix.

Effective behaviours, by contrast, are chosen by people above the line. They take on many different forms but share one characteristic: they're tailor-made to both achieve your aims and strengthen the relationship.

To check your normal default behaviours, do this quick quiz. It's time to awaken your Courageous Learner here. Imagine someone who knows you well is looking over your shoulder and keeping an eye on your answers. Just put a tick next to any of the behaviours below you recognise in yourself. If it makes you feel better, you can also do it for someone you're in a relationship with, ticking the behaviours they regularly choose.

The examples below are pretty extreme, so if you recognise even a tiniest whiff of a behaviour, put a tick next to it. Own up.

Aggressor behaviours

- Make your mind up about what you want, or what you think, before any discussion is had.

- Behave in an aggressive, disrespectful or angry way with people who disagree with you.

- Make demands and give ultimatums.

- Believe you're 'right'.

- Hold on to your 'position' even in the light of contradictory evidence.

- Ask leading questions merely to highlight why you're right.

- Pretend to listen to others while you formulate your argument.

- Appear to behave in a polite way while planning to undermine their argument.

- Blame others for how you feel.

- Resort to insults, sulking or tantrums when things don't go your way.

- Use 'absolute' language such as 'you never' or 'it always'.

- Try to beat down the disagreement or crush the competition.

- State your opinion over and over again (usually louder or more pointedly each time).

- Let them say their piece but then go straight back to defending your position without recognising the points they have made.

- Act hurt and angry if they say something you don't like.

- Tell them why they're wrong, and you're right.

- Bring up other issues that belong in a different conversation, but 'strengthen your case' in this one.

- Use phrases like "my position is" and "you just need to see".

Avoidant behaviours

- Avoid difficult conversations.
- Don't tell people what you feel or think when they ask you, but tell others behind their back or moan to yourself.
- Sulk when people don't do what you expect or want.
- Don't directly tell people you're upset but expect them to deduce this because you withdraw in some way.
- Make hints or sarcastic remarks about what you'd like others to change.
- Show others you're unhappy by being in a bad mood and expect them to drag it out of you.
- Give in or 'play nice', agreeing to something you don't want to do to keep the peace but then resenting it.
- Try and be tactful and polite even though you don't want to.
- Hope problems will just go away, so you don't have to deal with them.
- Get aggressive, defensive or upset when forced to discuss things.
- Worry about upsetting others if you say something they don't like.
- Blame others for upsetting you if they say things you don't want to hear.
- Stay silent until you 'burst'.

Effective behaviours

- Get permission to have the conversation in the first place.
- Agree a time that works for both of you.
- Clearly state the positive intent and purpose of any conversation, agreeing what it is before beginning.

- Share what you're both hoping to achieve as a result of the conversation.

- Share all relevant views and opinions, at the same time holding them lightly.

- Name the elephants in the room, i.e. bring to the fore issues that have been avoided to date and need to be discussed.

- Own your own behaviour in the room, respectfully holding others to account on theirs.

- Be big enough to change your mind if that's the right thing to do.

- Genuinely listen and ask more questions in order to learn.

- Have a greater need to understand than be heard.

- Ask genuine questions (as opposed to rhetorical or leading questions).

- Recognise that people are different and may not communicate in the way you prefer.

- Give people the space and time to talk.

How did you do? How honest were you about your behaviour in conversations? How courageous are you feeling? Why don't you give the list to someone you're in a relationship with and ask them to be really honest about your behaviour? And, well done – this level of truth-telling can feel really hard, but it's an essential part of the journey towards your extraordinary life. Hopefully, at this point in the book, you're getting better at seeking feedback without letting it rattle your self-worth. We're all works in progress, and this sort of self-knowledge is the only way to progress.

Remember: you can't change others

When we teach effective conversations on our programmes, we're consistently asked two questions.

The first is, "what do I do if I'm talking to someone who clearly has a bad intent?" The simple answer is, if you are not happy with the intent, don't have the conversation. Ask to take a moment to agree what the intent of the conversation is. Share what you think it should be and ask if that's okay with them. If they have a different take, either change it so it works for both of you or have two different conversations. Just don't move on until you've agreed a clear purpose and intent.

Here are some examples of what good intents look like.

For the couple that's always arguing: "I'd like to find time for a chat, if that is okay? I want to deepen my understanding of why we argue so much, so we can find a much happier way of living together. Would that be okay with you?"

For the team member who wants to work more effectively with their boss: "I'd like to find time for a chat, if that's okay? I'd like to find out what 'good' looks like for you in terms of my role, so that I can meet your expectations and understand the kind and frequency of communication you'd like. Would that be okay with you?"

For team members working together: "I'd like to find time for a chat, if that's okay? I hope we can both deepen our understanding of how we each like to work, as well as discuss our strengths and weaknesses, so we can get better results together. Would that be okay with you?"

The second question is, "what if I'm talking to people who don't know this stuff and they're being super-aggressive, so I look weak because I'm listening, being transparent and curious?"

The answer to this one is equally simple. We all know the outcome of two aggressors 'discussing' something: the biggest bully wins and the other feels dreadful. Similarly, two avoidants will either avoid the conversation or just skirt around the issue for a while, resolving nothing. But when you pair someone choosing effective behaviour with either an aggressor or an avoidant, the chemistry changes. When someone who is clearly above the line talks with someone below the line, they have a huge influence on the tone of the conversation, and the other person can't help but be influenced.

So there you have it: if you want to become great at conversations, you need to practise having good intent and choosing effective behaviours. Both of these things are 100% within your control. It doesn't mean that every conversation you have from here on in will go brilliantly, but it does mean the vast majority will be a hell of a lot better. And with every good conversation you have, you'll be one step further along the road to your extraordinary life.

RECAP

Intentional relationships

The quality of our relationships is the one of the most important factors in having a long, healthy and happy life. And remember, we have control, because relationships are created by the behaviours we choose.

- To build and maintain great relationships, we must get clear on our shared aspirations, and agree our expectations and ground rules for how we will behave.
- We must stay eagle-eyed around our beliefs and rewrite or let go of any that aren't serving us.

- Communication drives the energy in a relationship, so we must ask ourselves whether we want to be a Giver or a Taker, a Radiator or a Drain, a Cow or a Rhino.

- Effective conversations are the glue that binds us together. It's a learnt skill and one most definitely worth learning.

- Good conversations come from having above-the-line intent, teamed with effective behaviours; aggressive and avoidant reactions will only lead to deadlock.

- It's easy to fall into habitual roles in relationships, so knowing whether you're playing the victim, rescuer or persecutor can help you break unhealthy patterns.

- Even if others have poor intent or choose unhelpful behaviours, you can set the tone; improve your behaviour in a relationship, and the whole dynamic will change.

Proactive Wellbeing

"It is impossible to find what has never been lost."
Michael Neill

We were nearing the end of one of our Master Programmes, and I was about to deliver the final session. I swallowed two more paracetamol, tied my hair up in an attempt to cool my raging temperature, told myself "I can do this" and jumped up on stage. It went well. People laughed. People cried. The session required them to be deeply introspective. This was complex and demanding work, and I was proud to be part of their journey.

When it ended, I went straight to the loo and was violently sick. The irony was not lost on me; here I was, talking about Proactive Wellbeing, and this was the state I was in. When I got home the next day, I called a number I had been holding onto for months: the number of a coach I had a first session with months ago but had been too busy to continue with.

"I don't get it!" I burst out, cradling a hot water bottle on the sofa. "I love my work, I love my family, I exercise, I eat really well, I have regular massages, I never take antibiotics, I don't drink much, I never take drugs, I practise yoga, I'm generally really healthy but just recently I've been exhausted and now I think I have flu! I can't move my body – I literally can't move!"

She was very quiet for a long time and then said, "What's it going to take?"

"What do you mean?" I replied.

"What's it going to take for you to let your body do the work it's designed to do?"

"Sorry?" I said, not catching her drift at all.

"I've read your 'health story'," she continued (something I'd done for her, when we'd first got in contact). "And it conflicts with what you've just told me. I can see that you've had at least four bouts of flu in the last year – two lots of tonsillitis, constant headaches and, while you've refused antibiotics in the name of health, you've been mainlining cold and flu capsules, paracetamol and over-the-counter sleeping tablets."

That was the first day of my *real* journey into Proactive Wellbeing. It's a journey that I'm still on and will be on for the rest of my life. And it's changed everything.

Proactive Wellbeing – what is it?

Let's start with the word wellbeing. The media may have given you the impression that wellbeing depends on expensive yoga mats, organic kefir, scented candles, extreme workouts and exotic retreats (Instagram is especially good at this). But it absolutely does not. Wellbeing is, simply, the feeling of being well: mentally, physically and spiritually. It's a deep certainty that no matter what happens, we're going to be okay. It's an inner peacefulness.

When we're proactive about our wellbeing, we create the right circumstances so that our mind, body and soul can recharge. And it isn't about buying more stuff or starting crazy regimes. It's about getting out of our own way.

Why is it so important?

Well, think for a moment – what would your dream life be like without the feeling of wellbeing? Just imagine: even if you had the ideal house, job and relationship, if you woke up every morning feeling drained or demotivated, then what use would it all be? You may already know what I'm talking about. So many of us have experienced the crippling effects of poor mental or physical health and realised that, when we're in its grip, it's pretty much impossible to focus on anything else.

Just to be clear – I'm not talking about chronic health conditions or disabilities. These clearly need to be managed by a qualified physician.

I'm talking about the lack of wellbeing you experience when your inner calm or outer energy drops below a healthy level – for you.

This is the type of wellbeing we can ALL become more skilful at.

When we have the skill of Proactive Wellbeing – whatever that means for our unique individual system – life stops being scary and starts becoming an adventure. It empowers us to bring our full creative, connecting, curious selves to the world, and in turn inspires greater levels of success. Without wellbeing, we simply can't enjoy our achievements.

The three secrets of wellbeing

What's on your happy list? Go on, I know you have one. We all do, even if we've never admitted it to ourselves. What are the criteria that you believe, once they're met, will make you happy? A weight goal? A new house? A change in your partner's looks or attitude? The perfect job? A bit more sunshine? Less traffic? A smaller nose? A less annoying mum?

Most of us believe that, if we work hard enough at achieving everything on this secret list, we'll be happy. It's a game of effort, focus and hard work… and only the toughest, most driven will win.

But because it's impossible to control all the things on our list at all times, few amongst us get the opportunity to realise that the 'happy list' doesn't actually work. Those who do – those who get the house, the partner, the weather and the body they want – often just start writing another list.

Some, however, take a different tack and decide to examine their thoughts. They figure that if they're able to block all unhelpful thoughts and focus only on the positive, that they'll be happy. But this mammoth effort at self-censorship is not only ineffective, but exhausting too.

Now things begin to get tricky. Having realised that neither the happy list nor the blocking technique works, despair sets in. This is the place where I find so many of my 'super-successful', top-of-their-tree coaching clients.

The problem is, they've been looking in the wrong place.

Because here's the first secret of wellbeing. That feeling of contentment, excitement, curiosity, playfulness, love and engagement we all so desperately crave? It's already within us.

Secret 1: Wellbeing is innate

Being well is our natural state. We were born well. We were born happy. And then we got in our own way.

When I first learnt this, I was dumbfounded. It's so obvious, and I'd completely missed it! But watch any toddler playing with a box of sand or a bowl of water and you'll see they're overflowing with wellbeing (even if they have quite radical physical or mental challenges to deal with). One thing you'll never see is a toddler stressing about the size of their bottom in their nappy or cringing with embarrassment if they fall taking their first steps. No, instead they get up and have another go, and another, until they crack it. And the reason for this? They're unconsciously connected to their inner wellbeing. Life is an adventure; if they try something and it doesn't work out, they might shed a few tears, but then they pick themselves up and carry on. If they get ill, they rest until they feel better. Their bodies and minds do exactly what they're meant to do: they let feelings of discomfort pass through their system until they feel rebalanced.

And this is what would happen to us, too, if we didn't get in our own way. We could maintain our natural wellbeing if we stopped being scared of emotional or physical pain and instead acknowledged it, accepted it and allowed it to pass on through. If we stopped working to the point of collapse but instead listened and acted when our bodies needed rest, we would avoid turning a temporary moment of fatigue into a chronic state of stress. And, if we stopped ignoring the fact that our souls need attention too and took the time to regularly do things that make us joyful, happy, excited and energised, we wouldn't end up so fed up with the hamster-wheel of life.

We're born with an innate sense of wellbeing, but, as we age, pro-grammed thinking and habitual behaviours get in the way. It's like the leaning tower of Pisa. We all start off centred, happy and healthy – but as we slowly add contaminated thinking, contaminated food, drugs and destructive habits to our lives, we lean so far away from our innate wellbeing, we forget it even existed. We think our wellbeing will be found in that pint of beer, that new car, that joint, that miracle diet. Of course, we'll be perpetually disappointed, because we're looking for a solution that's outside-in, not inside-out.

When we finally turn our gaze inward, it's like discovering buried treasure. Slowly but surely, as we remove the layers of debris, we'll spot that glint of gold.

So here's the second secret of wellbeing.

Secret 2: You're always either moving toward, or away from, your wellbeing

How we think, behave and treat others and our body is either nurturing or destroying our wellness.

When you finally decide to try and reconnect with your spring of inner wellbeing, you'll need to be patient. It may take time to uncover the faulty thinking you've been hanging onto, and create some new neural pathways. But know this: your body and your mind are on your side. They'll literally be jumping up and down with joy as you get back in touch with them and begin to look after yourself again. They'll work in every way possible to support you.

So as you reach for that next cigarette, decide to stay at work instead of go for a run, tuck into another portion of fries or stare at a screen all weekend, ask yourself this: "Will this take me closer to or further away from my goal of wellbeing?" Pause and make a conscious choice.

And the final secret of wellbeing?

Secret 3: Wellbeing is an everyday job

Staying connected with the wellbeing of our mind, body and soul is a lifelong commitment. It's something we must focus on every day.

Knowing the true nature of wellbeing has changed my life. Despite this knowledge, and despite having lectured on its importance for over 20 years, there are still days when I neglect it or when I'm caught off guard (as the story at the beginning of this chapter attests). I can find myself lost in the illusion that my wellbeing is affected by things outside of me – whether someone's missed a deadline, one of my daughters is rude, the roof starts to leak or my mum's dementia seems to be getting worse. Literally, every day. And if I leave it long enough before reminding myself, I can spend days caught up in this outside-in illusion. It's like chasing my tail.

That's why this skill is called Proactive Wellbeing. Every day, we need to proactively focus on our wellbeing, consciously creating an environment that makes it easy for us to stay connected to our mind, body and soul.

MIND

We've already seen how important it is to choose the thinking that serves us best. But we also need to be able to let our thoughts relax and play. Let me explain.

Imagine you're busy planning your next holiday. You'll probably relish focusing your thoughts on the options available: studying the pros and cons of one hotel over another, calculating train fares, researching the best cafés. This is (unsurprisingly) called focused thinking, and it's very helpful. But you may also be letting your thoughts wander: idly daydreaming and enjoying the spontaneity of random ideas popping in and out of your head. That can be helpful too, not to mention a lot of fun. The problem sometimes comes when either your mind keeps wandering when you're trying to focus, or when your imagination veers out of control and you get caught in a thought spiral, leading to feelings of fear, anxiety and overwhelm.

To keep a calm balance between the two, we need to be able to access that old friend, our Conscious Mind.

When you sit in the armchair of Conscious Mind, you remember you are not your thoughts. You step back from your thinking and connect with the inner wisdom that sits quietly behind your mental whirl. You realise that even though you're brilliant at maths, you REALLY don't want to do it at uni. That even though the job looks brilliant on paper, it isn't right for you. That you're in love with your best mate and not your boyfriend. It's the place where your brain and body have the chance to tell you what you *really* want.

But how do you get there? How do you get to your inner wisdom? As an exasperated client once said to me: "I get it, I want to go there, for God's sake, I want to live there – but please, just tell me what I need to *DO!*"

The answer, rather annoyingly, is that we usually need to DO less. Instead, we need to create environments and opportunities where our minds can rest and regenerate. A list of things to DO to help you access your Conscious Mind will involve all sorts of things around stopping, slowing down and being quiet – and most people nowadays find that really, really hard to do.

Jenny Odell, the artist and academic whose book *How To Do Nothing*[15] has been a surprise international bestseller, has some powerful suggestions for why that is. "In a situation where every waking moment has become pertinent to our making a living," she writes, "and when we submit even our leisure for numerical evaluation via likes on Facebook and Instagram, constantly checking on its performance like one checks a stock, monitoring the ongoing development of our personal brand, time becomes an economic resource that we can no longer justify spending on 'nothing'. It provides no return on investment; it is simply *too expensive*."[16]

But if we don't take time to rest and recharge, the cost is far more profound. It will affect everything: your ability to think, to engage with others, to feel joy or excitement and to bounce back. Here are the three most powerful things I've found that can challenge our obsession with busyness and help us nurture our Conscious Mind.

1. Let go of your unhelpful stories

If you want to live from a calmer place and not get caught up in spirals, then you need to look at the stories you repeatedly tell yourself and others. The stories that are keeping you stuck.

When I met Maisy, aged 19, she told me that she hated her life. She told me that her parents had got divorced 12 years ago, she hated moving between two houses, and thought it was unfair that she didn't have a normal family. Her boyfriend was being horrible to her and she was convinced he was seeing someone else. Her brother hated her – which was fine because she hated him too. Basically, her life was awful – and, she added with a raised voice, "no matter what you say, I won't change my mind!"

A few days later I met Stuart, who was 26. Stuart told me that he hated his job, had very few friends and had a boss who was a liar and a cheat. He'd also fallen out with his father, who had 'made' Stuart follow a career path he never wanted; and, as a result, he never saw his mother, who he actually missed. For some reason Stuart believed that his relationship with his father meant he couldn't see his mother.

I asked both Maisy and Stuart how often they told these stories about their lives. After some initial denial, they both admitted that they repeated these stories daily – either to themselves or to others. I explained that every time they repeated these stories, they were reinforcing their belief (and strengthening their neural pathway) that their unhappiness was not their responsibility but was down to events or people outside of their control. In other words, they were living outside-in, and right at the bottom of the Ownership Ladder.

But before you judge them… pause. Almost *all of us* have a personal story that identifies us as a victim and keeps us stuck.

For many years, the personal story I repeatedly told to myself (and anyone who was prepared to listen) was that I was overwhelmed and stressed because I was building a business. I blamed my stress on my situation. I didn't want to face the fact that my stress had nothing to do with the business and everything to do with my thinking. I was unaware that I could choose to step away from my stressful thinking whenever I wanted – irrespective of how much work I had going on. The irony is that I now realise it's just as easy – in fact much easier – to be a happy, calm, busy person as it is to be one who is stressed and overwhelmed.

PAUSE AND REFLECT

What's the quality of your stories?

What stories do you regularly tell yourself or others?

Do you tell stories of how stressed/overwhelmed/fed up/unfit you are?

Do your stories blame a person or a situation for how you're feeling?

Who would you be without these stories?

Are you ready to leave them behind?

---

2. Rest and train your mind

One of the things we do on our programmes is ask people to commit to spending some time without distraction. An evening without music, social media, texting, internet, TV, books or conversation. We don't ask for a set amount of time; rather we ask what they're prepared to commit to. Most of the group are surprised when they realise how unsettling this request is. Some commit to only two minutes. Others relish the challenge and set more ambitious targets. But pretty much everyone, apart from the odd regular meditator, admits to taking no time at all in a normal day to stop and consciously still their mind.

Zero mental rest. When you think of it, doesn't it sound a bit… well, mad?

If we want our brains to operate as they're designed to, they need rest. Not just sleep (although they need that too), but conscious, wakeful, rest.

"While we were on the programme, the coaches challenged us to take some time one evening to rest our minds. People were freaking out, but I was intrigued. I think I was really keen to show I could do it. So I said I'd sit undistracted for two hours. Everyone laughed, and I must admit even I thought I might have bitten off more than I could chew.

"But I got home, ate dinner, explained to my wife and kids what I was going to do, then settled in. I'm not going to pretend it was easy. My body began to ache and my mind wandered all over the place… BUT I also found moments of absolute bliss. I felt like my mind was literally pressing restart and clearing itself. I lasted an hour and forty-five minutes then had the best night's sleep I'd had in years.

"The next day, my fellow delegates told me I looked different: that I walked taller and had a whole different, more positive energy about me. And it was all true. The other thing that happened was that when I woke up that morning, I knew I had to contact my dad. Our relationship had been strained for eight years and something deep inside me told me it was time to try and make it better. I called him that evening and we had a brilliant chat. We're getting together in a few weeks and I know this is the beginning of a new chapter. This is big stuff."

Luke, 30, orthodontist

In his book *The 15 Commitments of Conscious Leadership,*[17] Jim Dethmer shares research from NASA that clearly shows that if a person takes a nap for at least 30 minutes a day, they're 35% more productive than their competitors. He also points to research from innovation specialist William Duggan, which found that when we let go of trying to solve a problem, either through rest or play, the brain "recategorises and re-sorts all the apparently unrelated information into new, innovative solutions".[18]

One of the best ways to give your mind this sort of success-boost is through a daily meditation practice. This has the dual benefits of not only giving your mind an opportunity to regroup, but of strengthening the muscle of your Conscious Mind.

Contrary to popular belief, meditation isn't about stopping thinking, but rather about becoming the observer of your own thoughts. You can choose to lie, sit or stand. Begin by focusing on your breath – just one breath at a time. In and out. Watching the chest and belly rising and falling. Feeling the sensations of the breath. From time to time, you'll become distracted by a thought. Do you find yourself getting hooked by the thought? Caught up in a tangled mesh of thinking? Or are you able to see it as just a thought, notice it, then let it pass through you? As much as possible, choose the latter and return once more to your breath. It won't necessarily be easy and you may find you're distracted by your thoughts many times. Be patient. Persevere.

By becoming a better observer of your mind, you'll get to know yourself better. You'll observe the repetitive thoughts, the habitual worries and concerns. So that when you emerge from your meditation, you get to choose whether or not you want to make any changes to your life or take action to help your situation.

> **PAUSE AND REFLECT**
> ## Learn to breathe
>
> Take a moment to close your eyes and take ten deep breaths.
>
> Breathe in for one and out for two, in for three and out for four. Try to count to ten and then do another ten – that will be ten whole breaths. Each time you lose count just start again.
>
> See if you can make your breaths deep and long. As you breathe out, consciously relax the muscles in every part of your body – starting with the tiny muscles that surround your skull and ending in the tips of your fingers and toes.
>
> You will be amazed at how relaxing that is.

3. Remind yourself, daily

Let me say this again: despite having understood the importance of cultivating a Conscious Mind and living inside-out for many years, I still forget almost on a daily basis. This is infuriating, but totally normal. And one thing that helps me stay on track is to set aside time, every week, to re-learn and discover new research about Conscious Mind and the other Extraordinary Skills we are covering here.

With all the podcasts, videos and blogs out there, it's really not hard to make this a habit. You might decide to read a page from a relevant book, listen to an audio book whilst you wash up or walk the dog, or listen to an inspiring podcast during your commute. Where you find your inspiration doesn't really matter. What matters is that you remember wellbeing is an everyday job – and needs daily nurturing.

BODY

In 1939, Clara Marie Davis, a Canadian paediatrician, began one of the most ambitious dietary studies ever run.[19] Driven by a belief that 'body knows best', she convinced 15 unmarried mothers to enrol their recently weened children in an experiment run out of a local orphanage. In this experiment she set out to prove that when we take away the 'noise and popular beliefs' about what's right and wrong with regards to diet, the body will instinctively guide us and make the right choices.

Initially, it seemed that her hypothesis was incorrect, because each of Davis's test children, when presented with a whole range of different foods including over 30 'nutritional essentials', chose an individual pattern of eating.

"Every diet differed from every other diet, 15 different patterns of taste being presented, and not one diet was the predominantly cereal-and-milk diet, with supplements of fruit, eggs and meat, that is commonly thought proper for this age," she told her Montréal audience. Intitally this shocked Davis and her team – thinking that the experiment was doomed to failure. Yet, as it continued, over time what they saw were 15 completely healthy, happy, functioning children. While each child was eating a completely different diet, the result was that they were all healthy – in other words, they were all eating the 'right' food for them.

Questions were asked. How could this be? How could 15 drastically different diets produce the same results? The answer, Davis concluded, was 'Body Wisdom': that if you create an environment free of addictive substances, without the kind of programming that makes people believe that 'food will solve your emotional problems', then the body knows exactly what's best to do.

When we get out of the way of our body – and by this, I mean quieten the mind enough to hear what our bodies are telling us – the results are amazing. Clara Davis's approach has been updated and evolved into the 'Intuitive Eating' movement, which is currently making great headway in a world disillusioned with social media's outside-in idea of wellness.

But this doesn't just work for food. The 'Body Wisdom' approach is equally powerful when it comes to exercise, sleep and rest. Our bodies know what we need, and if we listen hard enough it will tell us, and then, we can make it happen.

1. Press reset

Of course, no one reading this book will have the clean mental slate of a recently weened child. Instead we have a whole web of neural pathways which means that, when we have a tough day, we automatically reach for the wine bottle, have a cigarette, place a bet, numb ourselves on social media or just do some more work. We may even have very real addictions that we need to overcome before our bodies are capable of sending us the right signals. Either way – now is probably a good time to press reset.

The good news is that pressing reset isn't about coming up with a ridiculous exercise regime, or a diet that you won't be able to maintain. It's about sitting back, taking a good honest look at yourself, and exploring the patterns, habits, stories and excuses you carry around with you in terms of your physical health. It's the first step in the personal change cycle we've used throughout this book – self-awareness. It's having the courage and patience to understand your current patterns of behaviour and thinking, and deciding whether or not these are serving you.

At the start of my own journey of trying to stay fit, I worked with a whole series of personal trainers… until I realised how much I hated gyms and would use any excuse to cancel. When I got quiet and paid attention, I realised how much I loved yoga, swimming and walking, and how I'd move heaven and earth not to miss any of those.

On my mission to have the body I thought I 'should' have, I tried every diet under the sun. And made myself miserable in the process. I even forced myself to eat meat (which I don't enjoy), skipped veg and ate minimal grains – desperate to lose the weight the diet book promised me I'd lose. Finally, I listened to my intuition and admitted that my body mostly enjoyed veg, salad, fish and whole grains. I also acknowledged my sugar addiction, and soon noticed that my system rarely asked for sugar unless I was exhausted. These days, when I feel exhausted, I try to rest instead of pushing on through, fuelled by sugar. Although I still do enjoy a piece of cake now and again!

PAUSE AND REFLECT

Learning to listen

Do you really know what your body needs?

Do you spend your life reading about what other people have discovered that their body needs – and trying to apply the same theory to yourself?

Or have you disconnected from your body altogether – overriding its demands for rest and recuperation so you can keep going?

How much rest do you actually get?

How much sleep?

How much time do you spend doing exercise you love?

2. Create a plan that actually works

How many times have you decided to change something in your life, only to find yourself a few weeks down the line having not just failed to do so – but feeling worse than if you'd never tried?

That's because most plans for change are literally designed to fail. They're 100% outside-in, consisting of following someone else's rules, buying whatever kit is required, perhaps sharing your plan for change with a friend so that they can hold you to it... a bit like trying to force a square peg into a round hole.

Hopefully, at this point in the book, you know that change requires you to start on the inside – and then translate that deep self-awareness and crystal-clear vision into behaviour.

What I'm about to share with you is a model for personal change of any kind.

Yes, this is big. This process is guaranteed to get you any change you desire – if you take 100% Ownership and commit to taking action, that is.

Let's pick an example and take it through the model to see how it works. Choose something about your physical wellbeing that you'd like to change.

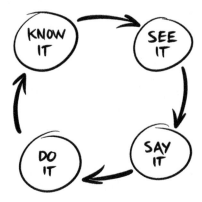

As my example I am going to use Charlie, who came on one of our programmes and was very concerned about his dependency on alcohol. He'd realised that he was probably out drinking on average six times a week with at least four of them turning into really 'big' nights. He never went out without drinking, and this was having a negative impact on his health and his relationship.

Step 1: Know it

The first step is to 'know it' – actually understand the situation as it currently is. What are the triggers for your behaviour, and what payoff are you getting from it?

Charlie found that his trigger was at the end of his working day when a colleague was popping to the pub. Being pretty outgoing and a good laugh to have around, he was pretty much always invited. So by saying yes, Charlie was in fact meeting his driving force for belonging. What most people don't realise is that every behaviour we choose, even the ones we think of as bad, serve us in some way. I know that sounds strange, but even the most seemingly destructive behaviours have payoffs. We may drink to excess to 'relieve' the stress we have created in our lives. We may work ourselves into the ground to get the recognition we so desperately crave. Before we can change a habit, we need to know how the current behaviour is serving us, so that we can make sure our new behaviour also meets this need – hopefully in a more positive way.

Honestly, if you don't understand your triggers and how your current behaviours are serving you, don't bother going to the next step, because the change simply won't work.

Ask yourself: What are your triggers? How can you see them for what they are (just events), and put some space between the event and your response? How is your current habit serving you? What's the payoff and how could you meet that need in a more positive way?

Step 2: See it

The second step is to 'see it' – in other words, actually visualise what you want.

In Charlie's case, he wanted to go out a couple of times a week and feel able to avoid alcohol on one of those nights whilst enjoying a couple of pints on the other. It was important to him to learn who he was without alcohol and to learn to enjoy his 'sober self'. Using the power of visualisation to support change is like adding rocket fuel to your engine. Research shows that the brain doesn't know the difference between what is imagined and what's real,[20] so when you visualise a new behaviour, you're literally creating new neural pathways in the process. Whether you're imagining a brilliant, fun night out without alcohol or imagining a terrible teetotal evening of boredom and isolation, you're priming your brain and your body to do exactly what you imagined when the moment happens for real.

Charlie committed to visualising exactly what he wanted at key points in the day – literally playing the vision over and over again in his head. He imagined declining invitations and accepting them. He imagined drinking soft drinks as well as enjoying a couple of beers. And it worked.

Ask yourself: What does your 'good' look like? Play it out in your head right now. Play it over and over again in as many ways as you like. Keep playing it in as much detail as possible to ensure you build that pathway.

Step 3: Say it

The next step is to 'say it' – yes, actually voice it.

It turned out that the thought spiral Charlie had been in repeatedly was: "I know I am going to give in and, when I give in, I will get blasted. That's just who I am. I am that guy. Anyway, it's not so bad, most guys my age end up drunk most nights. I can handle my drink – I never make a fool of myself. But it is bad. Shelly hates it, and she will probably leave me if I don't stop…" And on and on. One limiting belief after the other. And, the more he played it, the more he was strengthening the neural pathways to ensure that very response he didn't want, was the one he was getting.

We asked Charlie to create a new set of empowering beliefs – ones that strengthened him rather than weakening him. He then repeated them over and over in his head AND said them out loud whenever he could; programming his brain to make sure he responded the way he wanted next time the trigger came up.

Just to reassure you here – I'm not suggesting you lie to yourself. You need to repeat beliefs that are realistic and helpful. So, rather than saying "I'm teetotal," which clearly wasn't the case, he said: "I'm going to have a great night without getting drunk," "I'm going to have a date night with Shelly each week and have a lovely time," and "I still have fun with my mates when I'm sober."

Ask yourself: What could your empowering beliefs be? How could you remind yourself to repeat them? What will you commit to?

Step 4: Do it

The final step is 'Do it'.

I've always wished I could speak Italian… but, honestly, I've never bothered to put in the hours. I know I won't become fluent just by knowing, seeing and saying the words – I'd have to practise too. It's amazing how often we think this approach will work in other areas of our life. Well, it won't. To get better at something, we actually have to do it. The first three stages are essential to set us up for success, but *change* still needs *action* to bring it to life. So, whatever change you want to create, you need to do it – over and over again, until you get it right.

One of the best ways to do that is to enlist help. Tell people about the change you want to make. Join groups, find a mentor, get all the support you need. Then knuckle down and learn. Learn the new way of doing, and don't give up when you inevitably get it wrong or revert to the old behaviour because that, as we know, is all part of the learning process.

In Charlie's case, he was courageous enough to tell all his friends about his commitment to drink less. More than that, he asked them whether they would support and respect it. Most of his friends did help. As for the ones who thought it was a good laugh to try and persuade him to drink on their nights out, he simply stopped seeing them (that isn't exactly friendly behaviour after all, is it?). He also watched a number of AA videos online – having the courage to look at the raw facts about where he was headed if he didn't change. Finally, he decided to put all the money he was saving on alcohol to fund a weekend away with his girlfriend. The last I heard from him was a postcard from their trip to Copenhagen.

Ask yourself: What action do you need to take? How can you practise your new skill? Whose help can you enlist? When are you going to do it?

SOUL

Your soul is the deepest part of you – it's the part of you that makes you, you. Some call it your essence, others your spirit; whatever you want to call it, it's what makes me born to be a coach and you born to be a dancer, an accountant, a clown… It's why one of us adores lounging by the sea and another loves climbing a rock face. I know some people are turned off by the word soul, so feel free to pick a word you feel more comfortable with. But the truth is, connecting with that unique part of you – the part of you that is energised by certain things and not by others – is essential if you want to create a bigger, braver, more meaningful life.

The important thing about souls is that they need to be fed. When we feed our souls, it's like plugging ourselves into the mains and getting a full energy reboot.

Imagine for a moment you're doing something you absolutely love. For me that could be drawing or swimming in the sea. For you it might be cooking or riding a bike. Notice that while you're doing it, while you're in the midst of doing something you truly love, you're lost in it – focused on the activity for its own sake. In your element. Psychologists refer to it as being in a state of 'flow'. You're not busy thinking about your workload, your latest bill or that argument with your mother.

1. Find your element

One of the easiest ways to feed your soul is to spend as much time as possible in your element. And seeing as most of us spend the majority of our time at work, understanding what puts you in your element and trying to combine the two will pay off a hundredfold. Not just financially, although it's FAR easier to be successful at something you love, but in managing your relationships, taking care of your health… everything.

It blows my mind how many people I meet in the course of my work who are doing jobs they hate. This is often because of a limiting belief they picked up somewhere along the way that sounds something like this: "Work is hard, it wasn't designed to be fun, but I have no choice and I have to keep going." Or, "I can't become a chef because people from my kind of background don't do that kind of thing. If people are going to respect me, I have to make it in this job, I'll be seen as a failure if I stop now." What sort of a life is that?

The truth is that we all have the opportunity to find work that aligns in some way to our element. The difference is that only some of us are prepared to do the work to find it.

2. Live your LOVE list

A couple of days ago, I had lunch with a great friend. She'd just been out to LA for Christmas, where she used to live herself, visiting family and friends. Her Instagram was filled with pictures of amazing sunsets, canyon hikes, glamorous dinners and cool-looking people. When we met, she told me how lovely it had been to see everyone – but also how, after a few days of rushing around, she'd started to feel a bit disconnected from who she was.

She started to notice old thought spirals re-emerging and she was feeling edgier with people than she wanted to. "They weren't doing anything wrong," she told me. "I was just finding it all a bit much." The first morning she got back, she woke early, pulled on her wellies, and went to feed Albert and Star – the donkeys she'd recently adopted. She told me, in that moment, as she stroked the donkeys in the silence of the cold morning, she literally felt herself realign. She felt everything fall back into place and her natural equilibrium returned.

And that is the second part of feeding your soul. Discovering and living your LOVE list.

I want you to think for a moment. What do you love doing? What excites you? How do you love spending time? Write a LOVE list. Put everything on there. Here's mine.

Swimming in the sea

Great films

Yoga

Laughing with our kids

Photography, looking and doing

Family parties with games

Coaching

Chats with my brother

Experimenting with food

Theatre

Creating with the IH team

Meditating

Learning about people

Music

Cuddling Delilah (our dog)

Fresh flowers

Walking and sitting by the sea

Hearing Emmi sing

Weekends with my husband

Reading in bed

Art – looking at it and doing it

Long walks with audiobooks

Public speaking

Teaching

Days out with my friends

New cities

Writing

Sunshine

Having the house to myself

Dancing with my husband

Learning about history

Frosty mornings

Staying in lovely hotels

Deep debate with bright people

Watching Lara play lacrosse

Hot baths and early nights

Got it? Now the next part isn't rocket science. Print it out (yours not mine!) and stick it somewhere you will see it every day. Then make sure you do one thing, every day, that feeds your soul. Yes, every day. It could be as simple as dancing around the kitchen to a great song, cuddling the dog, a half-hour walk in the fresh air or ten minutes spent gazing out of the window with your phone on airplane mode.

See it as soul food, and make sure you eat regularly.

RECAP

Proactive Wellbeing

Wellbeing is the feeling of BEING WELL, mentally, physically and spiritually. It's an inner peacefulness.

- Wellbeing is innate: we were born with it.
- You're always either moving toward or away from your wellbeing. Be aware of your habitual thinking and behaviours – now is the time to challenge those that aren't helpful and substitute them for healthier alternatives.
- Staying connected to your wellbeing is a lifelong commitment.
- Mental wellbeing. You can still the unhelpful chatter and tap into your own wisdom by: letting go of unhelpful stories, introducing a daily meditation practice, listening to interesting podcasts/audiobooks or reading material that will keep you on track.
- Physical wellbeing. Make sure you eat a healthy diet (one that suits your body) and explore different types of exercise (and settle on one or two that give you joy).

- Spiritual wellbeing. Honour your own true nature, your essence, your spirit, by finding hobbies, by forming habits or trying new experiences that will make you feel true joy. Create a LOVE list.

- Know it. The behaviours we choose will serve us in some way – whether these behaviours are healthy or unhealthy. By understanding what we're gaining from our unhealthy behaviours – relief, relaxation, escapism – we can decide how to meet that same need in a healthier way.

- See it. Visualise the change you'd like to see. Remember, the brain doesn't know the difference between imagination and reality, so when you use the power of your imagination, you'll be creating new, healthier neural pathways.

- Say it. The stories we tell, the beliefs we repeat, all drive our behaviour – choose empowering beliefs and stories that create the result you want.

- Do it! Over and over again. And when you get it wrong – which you will; or revert to old behaviours – which you may well do too… get back up, recommit and move forward.

Human Leadership

*"Change will not come if we wait for some other person
or some other time. We are the ones we've been waiting
for. We are the change that we seek."*

Barack Obama

Navdeep and Corrine were both leaders in the sales function of a successful fintech business. Both were bright, driven individuals who had risen quickly to a senior level. They had both shown equal promise, but after six months Corrine's team was smashing every target while Nav's team, with all the same resources, was barely getting close. Worse, two of his eight team members had recently left.

When they both came to me for coaching, Nav was upset. He genuinely felt he was doing everything right, but he was nervous about his prospects in the company. So rather than analysing the processes each of them were following in infinite detail, I set out to discover if they were living from their Core Strength. Over a good few hours we talked through their visions, values, beliefs, driving forces, element and purpose.

It turned out one of Corrine's values was competition, which meant she thrived on having a target and an opponent to beat. Another was money – so having a big part of her salary tied to a bonus scheme worked really well for her. Nav, on the other hand, had a value of security and spent a lot time worrying about what he would do if he didn't hit his bonus. Another of his values was collaboration, so he found the competitive atmosphere difficult. It turned out his lower performance had nothing to do with his lack of ability or his lack of commitment to doing a good job. It was all about him not being in alignment with his Core Strength.

After gaining this insight and figuring out that he was really in his element when immersed in creative and commercial thinking, Nav moved into the marketing department. Eleven months later, he is not only running the team but being lauded as one of the most compelling and inspiring leaders in the business. From zero to hero in 11 months, all because in this new role he was firmly rooted in the person he really was and wanted to be.

So what does leadership mean to you?

A billionaire entrepreneur, showing off his latest product designs in a cool Shoreditch office? An arctic explorer, pushing the limits of human endurance to save his team from a snowstorm? A glamorous singer, performing in front of thousands of screaming fans?

These are all impressive examples of leaders… but they're just the most obvious. How about the girl who stands up for her mate when others are gossiping? The father who gently shows his five-year-old how to cope with her emotions? The quiet one on the graduate programme who works hard to make other people's ideas happen?

We all have the capacity to be leaders, in a way that fits the sort of life we want to lead. And if we want to live a life that's aligned with our core values, it's not just what we lead but *how* we do it that matters.

After all, looking at the world today, your idea of a leader is just as likely to be an untrustworthy, incompetent politician, a money-grabbing, climate-denying CEO, or a teacher who could make even the most fascinating subject feel like pulling fingernails.

Let's do a quick test. How many extraordinary leaders do you know? Take a moment and think about it. Think of leaders in your family, community, school, university, place of work – how many do you know? I've been asking this question to the people I work with for well over a decade, and in all this time, no one has ever named more than four. A lot people say one – and look pained as they struggle to think of that single extraordinary leader. Just as many say none.

This points to a bigger problem. According to a recent poll, just one in three employees trust the leadership of their organisation.[21] And yet, right now we've never known so much about what it takes to be a leader – there are blogs, videos and podcasts galore. So what's going wrong?

We're at a turning point in history. The old styles of leadership no longer fit. Needing to win, pursuing profit at all costs, having a game face, never admitting vulnerability… these are the behaviours that have led us into political extremism, social division, a crisis in the NHS, climate emergency and more. Leaders who spend virtually no time learning, changing, listening and collaborating are not what the planet needs for a brighter, better tomorrow.

They're no longer right for the new sorts of organisations we're going to see emerge over the next few decades, either. Power-motivated, dictatorial leaders worked fine when we were slogging away in factories or launching into jobs that might remain the same for 30 years. But they simply won't be able to keep their companies in business, or inspire others to follow them, in a future where technology keeps changing, resources are running out and environmental events are hard to predict. Authenticity, creativity, collaboration, agile learning and flexibility are already becoming far more valuable than the ability to shout the loudest.

Finally, those old leadership behaviours are making us miserable on a personal level, too. Interestingly, coaches and therapists are seeing their clients display the same toxic aggression and self-aggrandisement that some governments, businesses and institutions are parading on the world stage. Little wonder that mental health in affluent parts of the world is at an all-time low. A recent study showed that 85% of the global workforce feel disengaged with their work, and another discovered that in the past year, 74% of people in the UK have felt so stressed they have been overwhelmed or unable to cope.[22]

The good news is that the next generation – the people destined to become our future leaders – are demanding that things change. From Greta Thunberg and Malala Yousafzai to the guy at university co-designing his own upcycling business with his friends, young people are questioning the status quo and finding ways to lead and succeed in a more purposeful, meaningful and human way.

Do we have to work ourselves to the bone, neglect our family, destroy the earth and screw over our colleagues to make it to the top in our professional lives? Absolutely not – and it won't get you there anymore, anyway.

It's time to build a new sort of leadership, fit for our world and fit for the extraordinary lives we want to live.

Introducing Human Leadership

The final skill that's going to set you up for amazing success in your life is called 'human leadership'.

Everything we've learnt so far has helped you to become the leader of your own life. Now it's time to learn how to help other people to do the same. Because if you can do that, you won't just have a job; you'll have a lifetime of opportunities to make money, grow as a person and have a meaningful impact on the world around you.

Human Leadership – what is it?

Human Leadership is the practice of leading oneself and others in a way that empowers everyone to reach their full potential. No matter who, what, or where you choose to lead, it's about creating environments of meaning, growth, belonging and ownership; enabling people, organisations and societies to thrive.

For most of us, it's also about making a living. Many of us still want to have a nice house or car, to enjoy delicious food, to embark on exotic travels or to throw the odd party. But all the evidence shows that Human Leadership is also the most profitable form of leadership. Our current disengagement with the workplace is estimated by Gallup to cost the global economy $7,000 billion every year in lost productivity, and the only way to fix it is to change the way we approach work. So you don't have to choose between financial security, pleasure and meaning. Human Leadership is in fact the only way to deliver them all.

Human Leadership – why is it important?

It won't be long before the only jobs that haven't been automated or taken over by a robot or AI will be the ones that only humans can do. A recent report on the Future of Work 2030 suggested that in the next ten years, one in five jobs will likely disappear – and that the qualities which will be in demand will include the ability to teach other people, solve problems, read social situations, analyse systems and develop unusual and creative ideas about new topics.[23]

The leaders in this landscape will be people who can most effectively draw the human-ness out of those around them, whether face to face, online, or across time zones, cultures and social hierarchies. They'll reject the idea that the workplace is somewhere where you check your real self in at the door. They'll approach their colleagues as living, breathing individuals – not 'resources' – and consider their most important task not to squeeze every possible ounce of profit out of those people, but to help draw their unique talents out. They'll create work communities that will support people to experiment, fail, ask for help, learn, rest, celebrate and grow.

The what and the how

So how do you start to become a leader, let alone a human one? I've just Googled leadership and got just under 4 billion results in 0.49 seconds. That could take a little while to work your way through. I believe, however, that leadership is actually quite simple to understand when you break it down to the 'what' and the 'how'.

The 'what' of leadership is always the same. Whether you're the leader of your own life, the manager of an ice hockey team, whether you're on a mission to create social change or you're the CEO of a global organisation.

The job of leadership always involves three things:

• Having a vision that people believe in and are inspired by
• Having a plan that people trust will deliver that vision
• And creating an environment in which this can happen, both emotionally and in terms of process

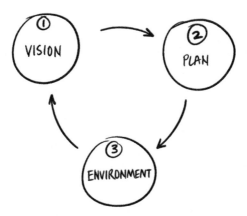

That is the job of leadership (the 'what' of leadership) and, whatever you're trying to do or whoever you're trying to lead, it's always the same.

It's the 'how' that really sets you apart from the crowd.

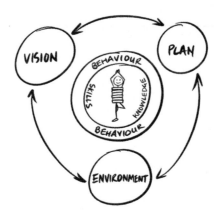

'How' you lead depends on who you are, the skills, the knowledge and experience you have, your value system and how you behave. In other words: how you lead depends entirely on your Core Strength, combined with your other Extraordinary Skills (100% Ownership, Conscious Mind, Courageous Learner, Intentional Relationships, Proactive Wellbeing). Think about Steve Jobs and Bill Gates, José Mourinho and Arsène Wenger, or Mary Berry and Nadiya Hussain – leaders who've been very successful in a mutual field but who got there using entirely different core strengths, skills and knowledge.

The truth is, you've already started on the path towards becoming a Human Leader. As you work through the questions in the previous chapters, you'll be building up all the self-knowledge and skills you need to be part of the change the future so urgently needs.

The rest of this chapter is quite focused on the world of work, because that's the sort of leadership for which most people seek guidance. BUT whether you're just at the start of your career, right at its peak or have opted out of the idea of a corporate 'career' entirely, I'd still urge you to read on. Think about how the skills and scenarios apply to the areas of your life where you advise, guide, support or work with other people (from being a parent or a member of a club). Human Leadership is extremely powerful, so don't ignore it just because you don't see yourself as a leader in the traditional sense. Trust me. If you want any sort of extraordinary life, you need to get good at this stuff.

HOW THE SKILLS YOU'VE LEARNT SO FAR ENABLE YOU TO BECOME A HUMAN LEADER

Extraordinary Skill 1: Core Strength

PAUSE AND REFLECT

Are you living from your Core Strength?

Take moment and think about any area of your life that's out of alignment. A part of your life where things don't feel right.

What do you think might be causing this? I'm asking you to look internally, not externally.

Are you spending enough time in your element?

Are you moving toward your vision?

Are you hanging out with limiting beliefs?

Are you violating any of your values?

Are you getting your driving forces met in positive or negative ways?

Rebecca was a prominent lawyer. She was the first female partner in her firm and the second highest revenue generator. She loved her work and really didn't mind the long hours. She lived in the house of her dreams and went on the kind of holidays that look like they belonged in a travel supplement. She had no children out of choice and was happily married to Jon, who was a very successful banker.

When we first met, it would have been easy to wonder why she'd sought out a coach. As she told it, her life was exactly as she wanted. So why did she need me? Our first few sessions didn't enlighten me much. She admitted that, for some reason, she had an empty feeling within her that she couldn't shake and was keen to be rid of it. She also mentioned that her team didn't like her very much, which 'slightly' bothered her. But she couldn't identify a reason for either issue. We went over every aspect of her life and she insisted that all was good. So I suggested I might talk with each member of her team to learn more about her and the relationships she had with them. She readily agreed. After a number of conversations, what I learnt, amongst other things, was that Rebecca was having an affair with one of her fellow partners. It had been going on for five years.

In our next session I told Rebecca what had come up and she looked really shocked. She wasn't shocked that everyone knew – she really didn't mind that – but shocked that this might have anything to do with her empty feeling, or how her team felt about her. "He makes me happy," she said. "Neither of us wants to leave our marriages, but it gives us the love and connection that we don't have at home."

Clearly, what Rebecca had been doing was meeting her need for belonging through her affair. This may have been okay for her if she didn't also have a strong value of integrity – which she'd been violating for five years. And because of that, her team, who respected her capability as a lawyer and a revenue generator, simply didn't trust her character. They instinctively felt that if she could deceive her husband so easily, it probably wouldn't take much for her to deceive them.

What Rebecca failed to realise is that the first job of leadership is to lead ourselves. To do this effectively we need to lead from our Core Strength, doing everything we can to stay aligned to our vision and values every day. She had an empty feeling because she was not tapping into the life force that empowers us when we're aligned.

Her team didn't enjoy being led by her because she was...

this person: instead of this one:

The job of a Human Leader is first to find out who you are at your core, and then do what you can to stay aligned. Of course, we all get out of balance at times, some of us more than others – again, this is a human trait, but Human Leaders are aware enough to recognise when this happens, know why it's happened, and do something about it.

Enabling others to live from Core Strength

One of the things we do on our Master Programme is get people to pitch an idea to a small group. On one particular day we had a filmmaker pitching an idea to a couple of execs from an international business magazine. It was a disaster. Mitch, brilliantly passionate, started to tell them his idea. After about two minutes they stopped him dead and asked him a series of questions – what was the purpose of the film? What benefit would it bring the business? How much would it cost and what were the other options for spending the money? Mitch stood dumbfounded. Even though it was just an exercise, he completely lost his flow and immediately began to doubt the viability of his idea.

The problem was that Vahay and David were analytical thinkers. They looked for facts, figures and evidence. But Mitch was a creative thinker. He didn't talk in bullet points or evidence his thinking. Instead he dreamed the impossible and sometimes, just sometimes, made it come true.

To run a successful organisation or team of any kind, we need people who think differently from us. People who bring different talents, and experiences and ask different questions. Recent research from Forbes found that an inclusive workforce is crucial to encouraging the different perspectives that drive innovation,[24] while a Boston Consulting Group study found that companies with more diverse management teams have 19% higher revenues.[25]

What this means for Human Leaders is if they're going to get the most out of their teams, they not only need to support others to find out what their Core Strength is, they also need to role-model embracing difference. They must demonstrate true collaboration – being more concerned with finding the best solution together than with being right. And they have to find ways of making effective communication part of the DNA of the team.

What Vahay and David didn't realise was that they needed Mitch's creative thinking in their business. They badly needed people who thought differently from them if they were going to make the changes they needed to make. If they'd been above the line, more open to learning during that pitch, perhaps they would have got the genius thinking they needed in their business, rather than shutting it down.

PAUSE AND REFLECT

Learning to embrace difference

Who are you shutting down at the moment, just because they think or communicate differently from you?

Where is it happening to you? This doesn't just have to be in work; it often happens with parents, friends and partners too.

Extraordinary Skill 2: 100% Ownership

Human Leaders take ownership for how they show up. They take responsibility for their behaviour and the impact they have on others. In other words, they sit high on the Ownership Ladder, recognise when they've slipped down and do something about it. They fully understand that events have no control over how they choose to feel and behave. They're full-on, stand-firm Rhinos.

Let me stop you right there! Stop and actually imagine that for a moment.

Imagine leaders who don't blame their team, the market, their boss, the government, the Tube strike or their bonus for the mood they're in, the behaviours they choose or the results they get. Imagine leaders who live inside-out as opposed to outside-in, understanding the unpredictability of life and not taking it personally. Imagine leaders who know that life is just one event after the other and it's up to them to choose their response and the quality of life they therefore get.

What difference would it make to our politics, our environment, our communities, our families?

And what difference would it make if those leaders also took 100% Ownership for helping those around them to grow, find meaning in their lives, and work in their element?

Human Leaders take 100% ownership of the culture they create

Elliot was a senior manager in a retail company. He'd asked for a coach because he was having trouble with his team. When I went to see him, he told me that his team rarely showed up on time to meetings and often didn't deliver to deadlines. On a recent employee engagement survey, they'd returned very low scores on their culture and environment, with multiple comments about feeling disengaged and undervalued. The solution, he thought, was to get rid of most of them and replace them with 'more competent' people.

I asked him to stop thinking about how he could change his team, and instead think about what he could do to change the culture he'd created. I asked him the question every underperforming leader should ask: what was it was about his leadership that had created the results he got? The problem was not his team; the problem was his leadership, and the toxic culture he himself had created.

On average, you'll spend 35% of your waking hours over a 50-year working life span at work.[26] It follows that how you feel during all those hours will have a significant impact on the quality of your life – not to mention a big influence on how well you work. A 2013 McKinsey study found that 90% of all managers identify the inability to generate a sense of meaning as the single biggest barrier to high performance.[27] So a poor or even just indifferent work culture isn't just bad for your soul – it's bad for business.

Interestingly, whenever I talk about this, a certain proportion of leaders inevitably begin to huff and puff. It's all well and good for charities and social enterprises to create cultures of meaning, they explain, but it's a damn sight trickier if you are an insurance company, a law firm or a manufacturer of industrial chemicals. The truth is, they have just as much of an opportunity – and a duty – to create a culture of meaning as their 'cuddlier' counterparts. Meaning doesn't just come from a world-changing crusade. It comes from a sense of belonging and a feeling of being valued; it comes from clear leadership, and from working in your element. Creating cultures that do just that is an option for any leader. It comes down to the choices you make on a daily basis, not the industry you're in (and as the 2018 Oxfam sexual misconduct scandal showed, toxic cultures are just as likely to show up in those crusading charities as they are in commercial firms).

You always have a choice whether to let someone play to their strengths or force them to conform to a tick-box list. You always have a choice whether to ask for feedback on your performance or see any criticism as a threat. You always have the choice to say sorry when you make a mistake or pretend it never happened. You always have the choice whether to listen to someone or talk over them; to change your mind or close it; to give others credit or claim it; to focus on long-term wellbeing or short-term profit.

One choice is Human, one is not. Every day, every moment, you have the choice. Make the right one.

> **PAUSE AND REFLECT**
> ## Taking ownership for leading
>
> What are you truly taking ownership for in your life at the moment?
>
> What are you not owning in terms of leading your life?
>
> What excuses are you using?
>
> What are you not owning in your other leadership roles?
>
> What excuses are you using?
>
> What do you want to do about it?

Extraordinary Skill 3: Conscious Mind

It was 10.20 am and Sylvie still hadn't arrived for her 10.00 am senior leadership team meeting. Her team sat waiting, catching up with work on their phones and making the odd wry comment about the state she'd be in when she arrived.

She was visibly flustered when she threw the door open. She swiftly instructed her PA to bring her a piping-hot espresso from the deli on the corner (it couldn't possibly be from anywhere else). She was only to be interrupted if Gerald, the CFO, called.

She then turned to the team, mumbled an inauthentic apology for being late, and proceeded to tell them why her coming week was about to be a blood bath. She ignored the agenda handed to her and jumped straight into talking about the damage limitation they needed to put in place to limit the impact of a bullying shareholder. She then told the team that she couldn't deal with anything else that day until the shareholder fiasco was resolved. She needed to avert disaster and simply couldn't focus on anything else.

Sylvie was caught in a thought spiral. She was totally lost in her thinking, convinced that the company was heading for catastrophe. She was already experiencing the pain of the fallout from the shareholder's actions... before anything had actually happened and despite it possibly never happening.

Let's just play that out again. All by herself, in her own mind, Sylvie had created an illusion of an unbearable future. She then decided to spend the next few days feeling the pain of that illusion. Self-inflicted pain that caused intense fear and anxiety.

A few questions:

- Does doing that – creating illusions of disaster in the future so that you can feel the pain now – make you happy? Well? Joyful?
- Does it put you in the best state to lead others?
- Does it put you in the best state to make decisions?

I used to do this all the time, before I discovered Conscious Mind, and it wasted so much of my time and energy. So why do we do it? I genuinely believe it's because most of us have never learned that there's another way. We've never learned that WE ARE NOT OUR THOUGHTS and how to access our Conscious Minds.

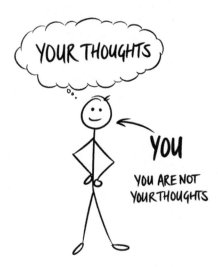

You cannot be a Human Leader without cultivating a Conscious Mind. You won't have the headspace to effectively lead others if you can't become aware of your thinking and let thoughts and feelings that don't serve you just pass through. Of course, you'll forget sometimes – I still do – and get caught up in some terrible, gruesome drama the mind has conjured up. But, by using our feelings as a signal, we are able to step out of the spiral and into that comfortable armchair where you get to choose what to let go of, what to focus on and what to do next. Because the brilliant thing about Conscious Mind is that it lets us apply wisdom to our thinking and feeling – allowing us to choose what to act on and what to ignore.

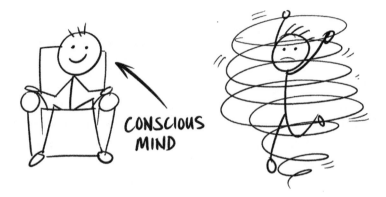

CONSCIOUS MIND

Human Leaders access their innate wisdom

The ability to step out of thought spirals and return to the Conscious Mind gives Human Leaders extraordinary power. Because when we quieten our thoughts, we are able to tap into the internal navigation system that we're all born with, but too often lose sight of because we're so caught up in our thinking.

Rani and I had been working together for a few months. He was a willing student and was keen to learn how to access his Conscious Mind. As part of his learning he'd embraced meditation, taking time for a 15-minute session every day. One afternoon he told me how much he enjoyed it. "It helps me to disconnect," he explained. "When I'm just there breathing, I can step away from what's really going on and lose myself for a few moments. It's a brilliant escape."

And in that moment, as Rani grinned at me, I realised that I'd totally failed to explain the real purpose of developing a Conscious Mind. I wasn't trying to help him escape. I was trying to show him how to engage – to engage with his deepest wisdom. Yes, it was important to quieten his everyday angst, but not so that he could 'disconnect'. The real aim was for him to truly connect with who he was and access the innate intelligence that had the power to transform his life.

If there's one thing I've learnt over the last 20 years of helping people build extraordinary lives, it's that success isn't down to how hard you work or how bright you are. True success – whole-life, whole-person success – comes to those who have somehow found a way to connect to their inner wisdom. They are the people who can easily separate themselves from their mental chatter and pay attention to the deeper voice inside. Most of us have been led to believe that the solutions to our problems and the answers to our questions lie outside of us, not within. But when we actually stop overthinking things, we generally *know* what to do.

While talking about innate wisdom on a programme one day, I noticed one of our participants, Adele, welling up. In the break she asked to chat and shared that she believed her inner wisdom was telling her to call off her wedding, planned for two weeks' time. She said that when her fiancé Laurie had proposed, she'd been swept along by the dream of a big wedding, buying a house and moving on to the next stage of her life and had tried to ignore the sinking feeling in her stomach. The feeling hadn't gone away and while she'd spent a lot of time telling herself it was just nerves, and rationalising that she was already 33 and needed to get on with building a family, she felt deep inside her that it wasn't what she really wanted.

As tears streamed down her face, she told me how she didn't want to hurt him or disappoint her family. Maybe it was just nerves? Gently, I told her that generally, the more reasons we have to find to justify a decision, the less likely it is to have come from our inner wisdom. I asked her to go home that evening, sit quietly with her breath and consciously let go of any physical tension. And from that place of stillness, I asked her to see what emerged.

The next morning, even I was astonished when she walked in. She looked like a different person. Not only had she done the exercise, she'd gone to see Laurie afterwards and told him how she felt. To her huge surprise and relief, he said he'd always known. And whilst he loved her totally, and would love to marry her, he valued himself enough to marry someone who truly wanted to be with him. Together they hugged, cried, laughed and in the end he thanked her for her courage as they parted. It was an extraordinary example of the difference that living by the principles of Human Leadership can make.

But what if I make the wrong decision?

When I share Adele's story, I get many joyful reactions; but I also get a lot of people gasping: "but what if she made the wrong decision?" Did you know that worrying over making the wrong decision is one of the most common forms of thought spiral?

Let's try a little thought experiment. Imagine that this statement was 100% true:

There are no right or wrong decisions. There are just decisions.

If that were true, how would it change your life? How much time and emotion would you stop wasting with endless pro and con lists, anxiety, second-guessing and stress?

Well, here's the good news: this statement is 100% true. Decisions are just that: decisions. They're not magic bullets that can make or break your life. All we can do is put ourselves in the best state for making them, opt for a course of action, commit to it, and keep adjusting our course according to whether or not it gets us closer to our vision.

But what does the best state for decision-making look like? I suspect (hope) that, at this point in the book, you know what I'm going to say. To get in the decision sweet spot, you need to genuinely listen to all the available data, and then get quiet. Let your thinking calm down and tap into the wisdom you have inside you. We've all had those moments of inspiration in the shower when our mind is quiet, and we can suddenly see what we have to do. We've all woken up, having 'slept' on a problem, and seen it much more clearly in the morning. That's our inner GPS talking – the problem is we're all usually so busy talking to ourselves that no matter how loud it shouts, we have no hope of hearing it.

At this point you may well be thinking, "Yeah, but… what about those times when I've got really quiet, I've waited for my wisdom to come calling, and I've heard nothing at all?" Well, in those moments you have two options. You can either wait a bit longer or just pick a path. If it's so difficult to establish the right path, there probably isn't one – just choose one and do everything you can to make it work. And, if after a while you find it isn't working, you can make a different decision based on the information you have at your fingertips. The important thing is, once you've picked a path, *don't* waste time indulging in the oh-so-fun game of 'post-decision remorse'. In other words, having made a decision, don't then get caught up in a thought spiral about whether or not it's right. I've seen this in clients over and over and it's the most pointless, energy-sapping exercise. Commit, act, recalibrate. That's all you need to do.

Human Leaders are people who've got super-familiar with their inner guidance system. That doesn't mean they ignore outside advice or evidence – on the contrary, they seek out all the raw facts – but when it comes to making decisions, having analysed the data, they put it all to one side and get themselves into the Conscious Mind armchair, get very quiet and listen to what they 'know'. Then they make a decision and move on. There are few circumstances when we know the outcome of one decision over another. But we also know that, as life moves on, evolves and changes, we can too. We always have the power of choice.

PAUSE AND REFLECT

Reconnecting with your wisdom

How connected are you to your inner wisdom?

How does it feel when you are?

What can you do to connect more often?

Extraordinary Skill 4: Courageous Learner

Sean was the founder of a new design start-up. Having worked in many dysfunctional organisations before, he was determined to set things up correctly right from the beginning, so he called us in to help him create a truly effective team.

We began by showing the team how to give each other constructive feedback, then observed as they took turns to form different pairs. After the third rotation, it was becoming more and more obvious that Sean was angry. His body language and his remarks spoke volumes – arms crossed, eyes rolling; "Yep, yep, yep," he barked. He was placing little if any value on the feedback given to him.

The atmosphere in the room was becoming increasingly tense and those next in line to give Sean feedback were looking uncomfortable. We called a timeout and asked for their feedback on the exercise. Everyone looked silently at the floor, inwardly praying that we didn't ask them. Finally, Sean stood up and said, "We're not children. If we need to give feedback, we'll just do it and move on. We don't need to waste any more time on this. I thought we'd be doing higher-level stuff." I asked Sean if he was prepared to share the feedback he had received in the exercise and he said, "Yeah. They think I'm doing a good job and are keen to get on with things. Oh, and there is some stuff on meetings."

The feedback Sean had actually received was that people were committed to the aims of the business but felt that they'd made a slow start. They felt his communication about the plan had not been clear and that it kept changing. They felt he dominated meetings and didn't get the value from the brilliant team he had recruited because he was always in a rush and rarely seemed to listen.

So, what happened? Sean – a bright, driven entrepreneur – knew that to succeed he needed an effective team. What he didn't realise was that to build one he needed to stay above the line, motivated by learning, as opposed to below it, motivated by being right. Moreover, based on the feedback about how he came across in meetings, Sean was unaware of his blind spots. In other words, he didn't know about all the stuff he didn't know. He wasn't just putting himself under impossible pressure. He was ridding his team of the chance to fully contribute and work from their element too.

Time and again, research shows that one of the most important skills for an effective leader is self-awareness. A recent study by the Korn Ferry Institute found that "leaders who are self-aware are more likely to be high-performing, to meet their business goals, and save on turnover costs."[28] Human Leadership isn't just about 'being nice' to people. It's about taking total ownership for yourself. In Sean's case, although he intellectually knew that it was a good thing to get some coaches to help him set up a great team, he wasn't quite ready to accept that it might require him to change how he behaved and perhaps develop some new skills (like meeting management). That's pretty common with people who've already got a lot of status and consider themselves a success.

But being a Courageous Learner is an essential part of being a Human Leader. It opens you up to change, growth, new ideas and collaboration. And it starts with an awareness of where you are – above or below the line. Again, it's not that Human Leaders don't fall below the line. We all do. But they need to be able to realise quickly, and swiftly realign. And of course, much of the time Human Leaders *do* know best for their business or their family or their community. They've risen to a place of leadership because they know what they're doing. They're often right. But the important thing is that they don't NEED to be right. And there is a world of difference between the two.

Human Leaders build learning cultures

Having the courage to look at the raw facts

Human Leaders encourage feedback of all kinds. They genuinely listen to those with a different opinion and are courageous in facing up to issues – whether about themselves, their team or a situation. But how are they able to look so courageously at the raw facts?

First, because they've detached themselves from the outcome. They understand that they've made a decision based on the data they had available at the time, they've got quiet and used their inner wisdom. And they know that their self-worth is not attached in any way to what happens next.

When I decided to set up Ivy House in 2016, a number of people told me I was mad. In essence, their response boiled down to: "You're crazy!

213

What if it doesn't work? You've had one successful business; you should just be pleased with that. If this crashes and burns, people will forget what you've done before and see you as a failure." To be honest, I was amazed at this reaction. What did it matter if the business succeeded or failed? I knew I'd put my best self into it. If it worked, I'd be fine, and if it didn't? Well, I'd still be fine. My self-worth wasn't up for grabs. This freed me up to take the leap.

Second, Human Leaders can face the raw facts because they master the art of being present. Ask yourself honestly: how often are you physically present in meetings, classes or conversations, but mentally totally elsewhere? I know. We all do it. But if you're regularly mentally and emotionally disconnected, how will you learn? If we want to look at the raw facts, we have to be present enough to see and hear what's really going on. Pausing. Breathing. Noticing. Tapping into our inner wisdom right then and right there, in the middle of life, not just on a summer holiday or yoga retreat. Human Leaders, like all of us, slip out of being present. The difference is that they make it part of their job to notice, then come right on back.

PAUSE AND REFLECT

Are you present?

Think of the last conversation or meeting you were in, whether with your CEO or your mum.

How present were you?

How present was everyone else involved?

What would have been different if you all had been truly present?

Self-coach, not self-judge

Remember this important distinction? Although self-judgement is a below-the-line behaviour, it can feel like the opposite. Surely this inner criticism is me learning? Surely this mental dressing-down is a form of ownership? No – it's you giving yourself a hard time for not getting it 'right'. It's you thinking that you've failed because you haven't 'won'. It's you getting trapped in a thought spiral of blame. And it only takes you further away from your innate wisdom; further away from the chance to learn.

Human Leaders understand that learning and changing are part of life. I mean they *really*, *really* get it. And this is *such* a rare quality. It's what makes them extraordinary. And because they know that life is a process of change, they relax about the whole learning thing. They don't push so hard. So many of us work so hard to constantly do things to 'perfect' ourselves, but when you realise that every situation is an opportunity to learn, you really just get on with living – knowing that *life* is your self-help course.

It's a much more enjoyable way of being, and it's also far better for the people you lead. Why?

Well for one thing, when you're genuinely motivated by learning, you avoid getting into the emotional and overwhelmed states of the constantly spiralling leader. When something doesn't go to plan, or doesn't turn out the way you wanted it to, you just ask yourself what you can learn. Once you've figured that out, you make the adjustments and move on, spending no time beating up yourself or your team.

And that's the second massive benefit. Because when you self-coach as opposed to self-judge, you also become a coach and not a judge for your team. If you're a judge, what are the chances of them hiding the stuff that goes wrong? High. You wouldn't believe the number of times I've been told about a senior leader, "She doesn't want to hear any bad news so be careful what you say." But when you create an environment where a key value of the team is to share mistakes and learning? Everything gets bigger, better and more meaningful, pretty fast.

Tom was clearly very angry when he called me. He told me that one of his colleagues, Carol, was out to get him and he needed a strategy that would both defend his position and knock her off her post. He told me that in their last team meeting, Carol had blocked his proposal to outsource one of his departments. She'd brought new information into the meeting that had made him look stupid in front of his boss, and he was fuming that she hadn't told him beforehand. Once Tom had calmed down, I asked him if he was above or below the line. He was quiet for a long time and then whispered, "below". I asked him to imagine for a moment that his only job was to take all the learning possible from this situation. If that were true, where would he start?

First, he admitted that he could have asked Carol's opinion before the session. She did have a lot of experience in this area. Of course, once he'd said that, he realised he could have done the same with the whole team. He also recognised he could have been far more open to hearing her questions in the meeting, and less aggressive in batting them down. But the big realisation was how attached he was to being right. What if Carol's idea really was better for the business than his own?

But Tom had no idea whether he agreed with Carol or not because he'd spent no time listening to her in the meeting and now was investing all his energy in self-judging. If only he'd got her on board before the meeting! If only he'd behaved better during it! What an idiot! For the second time that day, he was missing the opportunity to learn.

It's surprisingly common to spend your life thinking of all other people as tigers, deep down. But when we start to see every single situation as an opportunity to learn, we start to see everyone and everything as a friendly force contributing to our growth – rather than a threat we need to defend ourselves from. And breathe.

Holding opinions lightly

Remember Bill and Ben, who both believed they were unquestionably right?

Well sadly, most leaders end up headbutting like them, again and again. So one of the best ways to remember to stay above the line as a leader is to always hold your opinions lightly.

This doesn't mean you can't have strong opinions; of course you can. But you can hold strong opinions lightly, just the same. The minute you begin to confuse your strong opinions with absolute truths, you're on track for conflict, ignorance and blame. Instead, Human Leaders say things like:

"Based on what I know so far, I think…"

"Wow, you've got a completely different view from me… Please tell me more, what brought you to this conclusion?"

"This is my best guess… Tell me, what have I missed? Let's really stress-test this hypothesis."

"I don't really know what I think right now. I'd be keen to hear others' opinions to inform my own."

How much respect would you have for a leader who said things like that?

The minute people become determined to force their ideas upon others, they shut down their creative brains. They stop challenging and they stop asking questions. On the other hand, when leaders hold their opinions lightly, they're able to stay light, too. Flexible, agile, adaptable. They encourage cultures of sharing, of creativity and innovation, cultures that readily admit when an idea isn't good enough. And these are exactly the kind of lean, nimble, fast-evolving people and organisations that are going to thrive in our world of lightning-fast change.

Failing forward, fail fast

How much time is spent in your organisation trying new things? I mean genuinely *new* ideas. And before you even get to the trying bit, how much time is spent finding and discussing those ideas?

Chances are, less than is spent complaining about the coffee. You can probably observe the same lack of experimentation amongst your family or community groups. That's because most organisations and social groups run on a zero-mistake culture. Screw up, and you're blamed. And that leads to less and less creativity – and eventually less and less growth.

Remember the difference between the cultures of the medical and airline industries? One dedicated to uncovering and analysing mistakes, the other dedicated to hiding mistakes, protecting egos and killing hundreds of thousands of people in the process.

Human Leaders buck this trend. They share both their successes and their mistakes; they seek to understand why something worked or why it went wrong, and, importantly, they invite others to take a good look and see if they've missed anything. They create environments where it's easy for everyone to share and learn together, and those environments are what lead to extraordinary careers and lives.

Accepting you can only change yourself

For some reason, even people who understand that they can only change themselves in their personal relationships struggle with it when it comes to leadership. Surely part of a leader's job is to help people grow and develop? To help them change? Well, yes, it is... but you can't *make* them change.

Graham, a headmaster, called me in to talk about his teaching team. He explained that, while he had a small number of teachers who were truly open to learning and taking on new ideas, they were the minority of his teaching staff. The rest were made up of two other groups. One he called the 'fence-sitters': people who would do anything for an easy life, who never really got behind a new initiative but didn't oppose it either. Then there was the group he called the 'old guard'. He described them as bullies, not at all open to genuine learning or new ideas; he said they were often silent dissenters, spreading negative energy and criticism about pretty much anything new he tried to implement.

Graham's question to me was: "How can I make those two groups change?" My reply was: "You can't. You can only change you." I asked him, "What is it about the way you're leading that makes thinking and behaving like that okay in your school?" I pointed out that, by putting up with those two sorts of behaviour, he was making it okay. By not having conversations about what was really going on, he was pretending it wasn't happening. I challenged him to consider how clear his staff were on his vision for the school, the culture he was aiming to create, and the behaviour that required from everyone. How had he helped them become Courageous Learners? Become more skilled? Become less fearful of change? He began to realise that he couldn't change his teachers, but he could take an awful lot more ownership for the behaviour they believed to be acceptable in the school.

A leader's job is to create the environment for people to become their best selves. One of the most effective ways for them to do that is to show how they themselves are striving to fulfil their own potential. We need to role-model the behaviour we want to see in others, so, by showing them that we are constantly on a learning journey, they will be encouraged to be more open to learning. At the same time, a leader's role is also to hold others to account for their behaviour. While a leader can't change how their team think and act, they can decide whether they remain part of the team.

All of these factors usually require the leader to take their own de-velopment really seriously. I can't tell you the number of managers and leaders I've met who simply don't have the skills to do their job. Holding others to account on their behaviours is just one of those skills – one that only a few of us learn in the course of our work. It's an example of how Human Leaders must always stay alert to how much they still don't know and keep finding ways to plug the gaps.

For some reason, the more successful someone is within an organisation, the *less* time they spend on their own development, the *less* feedback they get, and the *less* they're challenged. When you think about this, it's crazy. It should be the opposite. But many senior leaders seem to believe they're too busy for leadership development or coaching. They see their learning as keeping up to date with what's going on with the markets, their sector or their competitors, but give no time or attention to their behaviour or people skills even though it could have a significant impact on the success of their organisations and their lives. The whole system is topsy-turvy, and it urgently needs to change.

The list of specific skills that each leader needs to develop is influenced by the nature of their job and the skills they already have. On our programmes we get people to work on their skills map so that they're clear about the skills they have, the skills they're actively working on, and the skills they want to develop in the future. I've listed just a few of the most common ones below.

How skilled are you in each of these areas right now? Remember, this doesn't just apply to the workplace. You'll need some of these skills to improve your relationships with your family, friends, neighbours and acquaintances too.

Creating effective teams	Managing effective teams
Meeting management	Effective conversations
Personal pitching	Telling compelling stories
Presentation skills	Influencing others
Networking	Giving behavioural feedback
Coaching	Giving clear briefs

PAUSE AND REFLECT

What are you really good at?

How clear are you on your skills? This will be crucial to not only understanding your potential value as a leader, but to mapping your development.

What skills have you already mastered?

What skills are you actively developing currently?

What skills will you develop in the future?

Extraordinary Skill 5: Intentional Relationships

A recent Danish study suggested that more than half of people who leave their jobs do so because of bad management.[29] Human Leaders understand this, so they don't leave their relationships to chance.

As you already know, all relationships are created by the behaviour we put into them. This is no different when it comes to leadership.

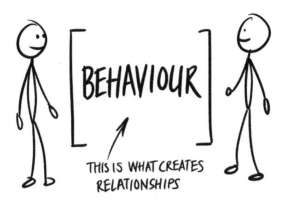

However good a leader's intentions, cause or vision, if the behaviour they choose to put into their relationships is aggressive, dismissive and arrogant, then that's the sort of leader they are. So what kind of leader do you want to be? And what does that mean for the behaviour you're going to have to choose? Just to be crystal clear here – I'm not suggesting you choose 'fake' behaviour to influence others, increase your status or get certain results. That might work in the short term, but it's unsustainable. In this journey, we're focusing on behaviours that will keep you successful and happy *for life*. You need to pick behaviours that represent the best of your natural leadership qualities – behaviours that you can reproduce every day. Because without consistency, you won't get any trust.

As a leader, you will be judged by your character AND your competence

People experience you through your behaviour – so it's through this behaviour that they'll decide whether they want you as a leader in their business (or local group, or activist organisation, or social media feeds, or simply as someone they'd speak highly of). Ultimately, they're deciding whether they trust you, even if they've never met you in person.

In her book *Presence: Bringing your boldest self to your biggest challenges,*[30] Harvard psychologist Amy Cuddy reports that people instinctively ask themselves two questions when they meet someone new. The first is, "Can I trust this person?" and the second is, "Can I respect this person?" These two criteria – otherwise known as character and competence – are crucial to establishing Human Leadership.

Jade and Rob were part of a leadership audit we did for a media conglomerate. Jade was a lovely person. You could just tell. She always checked in with how her team were doing, conscious of not wanting them to get too overwhelmed with the transformation project they were heading up. She made sure she gave them the recognition they deserved, and they trusted her loyalty to them in front of the senior management team.

But the problem with Jade was that she wasn't competent in a number of crucial skills necessary for her role. Her team said her meetings were 'disastrous': always running over time and never delivering the clarity they so desperately needed. They also said she lacked the skill to engage the wider team when they were all together, reporting that her presentations were boring and lacked inspiration. "We really like her," they said. "She's a lovely person – she just isn't very good at her job."

Rob, on the other hand, seemed to have developed a great skill set. He ran effective meetings, gave really clear briefs, held people to account on timings and delivered presentations that were factual, engaging and inspiring.

The problem was people didn't really like him. His team said they didn't know him very well because he never shared what was going on for him or what his life was like outside of work. They said he clearly didn't believe in being friends with colleagues and, while they respected his choice, it meant that they didn't feel connected to him at all. Somehow this meant that work felt less meaningful. They didn't really feel like they belonged to a team, and felt like they were a collection of polite strangers getting on with the job.

There's a clue in the title. Human Leaders lead human beings. And because the quality of our feelings determines the quality of our lives, human beings want to feel genuinely connected to their leaders, as well as having faith in their ability to do the job. Even if you think you're just in a role to make money, I can guarantee that deep down you want to be seen and valued by your leaders, and to play a genuine role in helping the organisation achieve its goals (and if you don't, you need to find a different role).

Sadly, this understanding has passed many of our current leaders by. It probably wasn't helped by the introduction of the term 'human resources'. Coined in the United States in the mid-20th century, as capitalism was skyrocketing after the war, this term put people in the same camp as other resources that help an organisation succeed, such as raw materials, finance and technology. This made it easier for businesses to quantify the contribution and cost of their staff, but neglected their humanity. It encouraged us to believe that less quantifiable human attributes, like emotions, talent, creativity and relationship-building, were not just less important, but sometimes irritating when it came to running a smooth commercial machine.

Research shows that, when we separate our 'personal' selves from our 'professional' selves, everyone loses out (including the business). One recent study from Gallup showed that employees who claim to have had meaningful conversations with a manager about their goals and accomplishments are 2.8 times more likely to feel a sense of commitment to their jobs.[31] And as we saw from the Future of Work 2030 study[32] I mentioned at the start of this chapter, relationship-based skills like collaboration, innovation and creativity are becoming the most sought-after qualities in a highly automated, rapidly changing marketplace.

So, we need to create a shift. A proper shift. A shift where leaders recognise that by putting themselves up for leadership positions, they're putting themselves up for not only being experts in their subject, but also for being experts in relationships. Relationships in which they will be judged on their behaviour, however senior they are within the organisation. Relationships that require them to bring their whole selves to work. Relationships that mean they must understand and care for the people around them, share their own strengths and weaknesses, and take ownership for continually analysing and improving their own skills.

To understand why this is so important, just look at the ways in which inhuman leadership has impacted our world today, from social inequality to COVID-19 to the climate crisis. Being a leader of others is a huge responsibility, whether you're a community leader or the leader of a large organisation. Do it badly – or unconsciously – and you can do real damage. But do it well, and you can change the world of many that you meet.

You are one person

One of the things we get asked about regularly on our programmes is this idea of being one person at work and another at home. Our answer is always the same. You are one person. You may be choosing to only bring one part of you to work and hide the other bits of you, but you are only one person. For some reason, so many people believe that to be successful in work they have to hide their 'true' personality, believing that if their colleagues knew who they 'truly were', then they either wouldn't like them or their future career path would be hampered in some way. When you think about how many hours we spend at work, this is truly tragic.

One Life, the 2018 book by the philosopher and business executive Morten Albaek,[33] is superb in this regard. As he puts it: "Of course, we have different roles associated with different responsibilities, but we are never different people. We are one person when at work and at leisure. The worker, the parent and the sibling are the same person […] we have conned ourselves into thinking that work isn't existential, but merely a practical requirement given form by a profession. Unfortunately, however – or perhaps fortunately – our minds and bodies are so primitively wired that they don't understand this division."

One Saturday morning as I was wandering through Soho with my husband, we passed a tiny gallery. With time on our hands, we popped in and were treated to the most incredible display of mixed-media art I have ever seen. Excited, we tentatively asked about prices to see if we could afford a piece. The assistant said we were in luck, as the artist was in the back room. Did we want to meet him?

When Saul came out of the back room, I was pleasantly surprised. I knew Saul! He was a leader at one of the engineering companies I was working with. From the look on his face, Saul was equally surprised – but not in a good way. As he approached, the first thing he said was: "Please don't tell them! I do love my job. This is just my hobby."

Intrigued, I persuaded Saul to leave the gallery and join us for a coffee. He told us about how he believed that he had to be a certain way to be a project manager – and how this side of him, the 'creative Soho artist', wouldn't be understood or valued in the firm. I asked him how he felt keeping this 'other life' from the people he worked with. "Exhausted," he told me. "Exhausted and a little sad."

He admitted that he'd been delighted to get this exhibition and would have loved to invite people from work, but he'd feared it was inappropriate and worried about how they would view him afterwards. I then asked him how connected he felt his team were to him. "Not really at all," he sighed. "We have some good banter, but they don't really know me, the real me, do they?"

How do you feel when others hold back on you? How connected do you feel when others don't share what they care about, and what's going on in their lives? The truth is we can't connect to others unless we have something to connect *to*. Sharing experiences, dreams, challenges, thoughts and feelings is what builds relationships. Take that away and what do you have?

But choosing to bring your whole self to your leadership role isn't always easy. It means accepting three tricky things.

The first is that not everyone is going to like you… and you're not going to like everyone else. We all have a unique set of preferences, and some just clash. But honestly, accepting this is SO freeing. It's made a huge difference to my life. When you stop trying to get others to like you and instead focus your energy on being someone *you* like, you're able to form genuinely meaningful relationships with people of all kinds.

Second, human beings want to work for other human beings. They don't want to work for superheroes, however much you feel it's important to put on an invincible front. They want to see *you*. They want to hear you admit your mistakes, have you share what you're working on and watch you celebrate what you're proud of – because when you do that, you give them permission to do so, too. And when we show up as ourselves, and make it okay for other people to show up as themselves, we clear the way for us *all* to have extraordinary lives.

Finally, working with people in a human way does require you to build friendships. I'm not talking about becoming BFFs with your finance director or going on holiday with your intern, but I am talking about caring for each other, taking the time to get to know each other and helping all the real, living, breathing, loving, hurting, hoping individuals within your team create a work environment that works for them.

Andy is a crucial member of the Ivy House team. Outside of work, he's a passionate cyclist and has won two silver medals and one gold medal at the Invictus Games. Cycling almost every day keeps him fit and happy, but that doesn't fit with 'normal' working hours, especially in the dark mornings and evenings throughout the winter months.

It was easy for us to agree that Andy could start at 7 am each morning and leave work in the evenings in time to go for a ride (and sometimes pick up his daughter, too). Of course, now and then Andy needs to be at one of our evening events and has to miss a ride or pick-up. But most of the time it's perfectly easy for us all to flex, and it's more than worth the effort. This simple act allows Andy to have a job he loves, continue his passion for cycling, and be a good dad. And for the business, it means we get an incredibly committed, high-performing operations manager – not to mention a happy and healthy friend.

Using the ABC in leadership

Given the importance of relationships in leadership, it makes sense to invest some time and effort in figuring out how to get them right. The great news is that you've already got all you need to do so: the ABC of relationships.

Aspiration and Agreements: Having clarity about what kind of relationship you're each aspiring to – and therefore what agreements need to be in place – clears up many of the issues that commonly play out between leaders and their team members.

Beliefs and Behaviours: It's also crucial to have a good think about any beliefs you're carrying that may be getting in the way of a leader–led relationship, and the behaviours you each need to put into the relationship to achieve your mutual goals.

Communication and Conversations: Being clear on your general communication and the intent of your various conversations will make all the difference.

Of course, most people are frightened by the prospect of saying to their boss: "I'd like to have a conversation about how we create the best relationship we can." My advice? Decide who you want to be.

"When I learnt the ABC of relationships, I knew I had to have a conversation with my boss. We'd been working together for nearly a year and, on the face of it, all seemed fine. We were quite matey and would often go for a beer together. But the reality was that at work, there was a fair bit of tension between us.

"I was fed up that he often made big promises that he didn't follow up on; he never gave me constructive feedback, and I had a sneaky feeling that he wasn't always complimentary about me in the office. I couldn't put my finger on it, but I just didn't totally trust him. The problem was that we 'pretended' it was all fine; we were two blokes that didn't 'do' deep and meaningful conversations and it all just felt a bit embarrassing.

"When I spoke to my coach about this, he asked me two questions. The first was: 'How important is it to you to get this right?' I realised that getting this relationship right was really important. It was starting to affect how I was feeling about work, and that was affecting how I was feeling at home. Also, I knew I needed my boss to support me when I went for the promotion I wanted.

"The second question really hit me though: 'Who do you want to be?' That was tough. Did I want to continue avoiding the conversations – accepting how I was feeling, being a bit of a coward – or did I want to step up and own it? I decided on the latter.

"I'm not going to lie to you; it was a bit cringy at first, but when we got into it, it was brilliant. He actually admitted to not being fully supportive of me and told me why. Which means I now have an honest view of what I need to do and, he's agreed to doing what he says he will. A load more came out of it other than that but most importantly I feel stronger than I ever have before by taking action."

Lewis, 22, senior analyst

Teams – the collaborative relationship

One of the most crucial relationships a leader needs to get right is the relationship with their team. Because it's made up of a series of individual relationships, it's useful to think of a team as an organisation in its own right. Be very intentional about how it is created, too. After all, there's a massive difference between an effective team and a group of people that happen to work together.

Here's a fact: teams outperform individuals. We can do more working alongside other people than we ever can alone. Of course, some work requires isolation and teams can't solve every problem, but they're undoubtedly needed at some point for anyone who wants to achieve ambitious goals.

So why then – when we're exposed to so much content about what makes a great team, and when we're inundated with shiny platforms and apps promising to revolutionise teamwork – aren't we being bowled over by the extraordinary performance of teams in business, politics, sports and more? A 2015 report from the Center for Creative Leadership called 'The State of Teams'[34] found that the majority of team members across different industries experience struggles with resolving conflict, coordinating activities, and constantly changing memberships, while only about 50% of leaders believe their team exceeds organisational expectations.

The fact is, we've spent most of our lives learning, living and surviving as individuals. When we did a test at school, we compared our marks with those of our friends. When we ran a race, we aimed to win. When we entered the world of work, we learnt that success involved delivering against our personal objectives and striving for promotion against our colleagues. From a very early age, so much of our focus has been to compete, lead and succeed… alone.

So, when we're suddenly asked to put the team first, to trust in others and make our success dependent on multiple people, it's frightening. And what adds to this fear is that very few people have experienced the feeling of being part of an extraordinary team.

Then there's the fact that creating effective teams requires time, focus and commitment. It very rarely 'comes naturally' – it's a learnt skill, which requires both leader and team members to pull their weight. And above all, it requires a clear understanding of what your team is *for*. 'Being a great team' is not the goal. Achieving something tangible, and feeling good while you do it, is what you're all there for.

So please, don't apply all the Extraordinary Skills in this book to yourself as an individual, then dump them by the wayside in your behaviour within a team.

To achieve all the things you want to achieve, you need to be part of an extraordinary team. To make the kind of wholesale change we need in the world, we need powerful teams. As a Human Leader, they're your ultimate (positive) weapon. Arm up.

Extraordinary Skill 6: Proactive Wellbeing

How many leaders do you know who proactively look after their wellbeing? All of it – mind, body and soul? Leaders who take time out of their day to meditate or go for a run, who read books that inspire them, who eat a proper lunch, who rest?

Probably not many, I'm guessing. But imagine the difference it would make if the leaders in your life (other than yourself) did this stuff. What impact would it have? What difference would it make to how they show up to their role? How would it alter their ability to handle change, to provide clarity and to connect with others?

Everything we've talked about so far in terms of becoming a Human Leader – the ability to choose your behaviour, the skill to step out of your thinking, the courage to keep learning, the energy to connect with others… all of this is dependent on you being 'well'.

Our wellbeing is (literally) at the core of our extraordinary lives. It's what makes us, us.

But so many leaders forget this. They get caught up in the illusion that the most important thing they need to do is whatever's on their to-do list. They see themselves as machines, as 'resources' that just need to keep producing more – faster, and better. And when they do this, disaster awaits – not only for them, but the cultures they create, and the planet they live on.

Busyness

Having spent so many years working with senior leaders, I've spent many hours listening to people justify their need to be busy 24/7, often to a degree that breeds health-threatening stress. What's shocked me over the last couple of years is that, through my work with emerging leaders, I've come to realise that this toxic aspect of our culture is by no means diminishing – I suspect it is in fact worse than ever before. It doesn't help that, unlike their Baby Boomer predecessors, Millennials and Gen Z-ers have been brought up in schools which, in many ways, replicate the high-pressure environments of the organisations they aspire to join.

A recent survey revealed the shocking statistic that more than a fifth of 14-year-old girls in the UK have self-harmed.[35] A YouGov survey found that one in four students suffer from mental health problems.[36] And the Health and Safety Executive reports that work-related stress, anxiety or depression accounts for over half of all working days lost due to ill health in Great Britain.[37] How bad do these stats need to get before someone realises that the way we're approaching work right now isn't working?

Workaholism is an addiction. Like any other addiction, it's a behaviour we feel compulsively drawn to do, over which we believe we have no choice. You might call repeatedly checking your phone, continually refreshing emails, taking work calls wherever you are, thinking about work constantly and working to exhaustion 'being busy'. I call it something else.

What's doubly interesting is that, although chronic busyness is an addiction, with all the truly harmful effects of an addiction, in many circles it's seen as positive. In fact, many people are proud of what they see as their super-powered work ethic and judge those who take a more balanced approach as weak.

This is – excuse my language – damaging bullshit. Damaging to us, to others, to organisations, to societies and to the world.

Living an extraordinary life is not about surviving, and constantly striving. It's about achieving great things, yes, but it's also about rest and fun and calm.

"When I got the job at one of the top law firms, I was over the moon. But two years in I couldn't cope. Every morning I'd get up in a half-dead state, get on the Tube, grab some breakfast on the way to work, and inhale God knows how much coffee to get me through the morning. I'd work in a state of palpitation-inducing anxiety, until at some point in the evening when I couldn't function anymore, I'd leave to take the Tube home. Most evenings I ate takeaway, then spent what was left of the evening self-numbing with drink, drugs, and mindless online surfing. I'd then sleep (badly) and repeat. By the time the weekends came I was so exhausted (and I realise now, a bit depressed), I had no energy for a social life. I'd go to the gym because I knew I needed to exercise, and that was about it. At least half of every weekend I worked to just keep up with the workload, and I honestly can't say what else I did. I was brain dead.

"It ended in what I can only see now as a bit of a breakdown. I got flu one week, so bad I couldn't get out of bed, and it just went on and on. The thought of going into work, even as I started to recover, became more and more frightening. What I realise now – with the benefit of hindsight – is that I'd put my wellbeing so low on my priority list, it had completely dropped off. But I also realise that the culture within my organisation, while it claimed to care about our wellbeing, in practice didn't at all. The partners had a sink-or-swim attitude to trainees. They believed that only the strongest would survive – and those were the ones they wanted. They actually recruited the brightest, most driven young people and tried to break them. What kind of culture is that?

"Finally, after I recovered and went back to work, I realised that rather than being weak, the strong thing to do was really to stand up and say I didn't want to be part of this bullying, inhuman culture anymore. I went to see the managing partner and asked if he wanted to create change in the organisation. He didn't, so I left. And when I interviewed with the new firm I'm in now, I had some very different conversations from the ones I had the first time round. Sometimes, as Gandhi said, you have to 'be the change you want to see in the world'."

Brad, 28, lawyer

Proactive Wellbeing is at the heart of Human Leadership. It's about recognising that people want to see their children's school concert, they have dentist appointments, they need a social life and they crave time to lose themselves in their hobbies. It's about trusting in the goodness of people, and knowing that when we're kind and flexible, they repay us tenfold. You cannot buy the loyalty and dedication that approach brings you – and it makes all the difference when a crisis hits.

Extraordinary Skill 7: Human Leadership

Human Leadership, then, is the culmination of all the other Extraordinary Skills. It asks us to understand ourselves deeply, constantly learn and grow, and lead others by leading ourselves to become the person we want to be. All of this is what I would call internal work. So I want to end by looking outwards, showing you how to create a powerful, authentic, influential brand as a Human Leader.

Now before you slam the book shut, I can reassure you that there is not one whiff of cynical, shiny, social-media-influencer-style posturing here. When I talk about your brand, I mean one that truly represents you; one that allows others to see you for the brilliant person you are, and allows you to make the greatest possible impact on the world. Even that might make you feel uncomfortable, but that's exactly why you need it. Because without a strong brand, your own unique kind of extraordinary simply won't cut through all that ordinary noise. And we need it to.

When I met Caroline, she was angry. She'd been with the publisher she was employed by for 17 years. She'd never taken a day off sick, eagerly taken on multiple new projects, always delivered on time and on budget, run six different departments, and knew the intricate workings of the business like no other. But in the last three years there had been three new appointments to the senior leadership team, and no one had even spoken to her about attending an interview. I met Caroline at a party just as she'd decided to hand in her notice.

As we chatted, I asked her to imagine she was her CEO for a moment. How would the CEO describe 'Caroline'? What adjectives would she use? Caroline looked at me blankly and said, "I have no idea – how would I know?" You may not be surprised, at this point, to hear that I pushed. Come on, what might she say? She finally came up with: "Loyal, trustworthy, hard-working, quiet." "So, do you think that's the sum total of your brand?" I asked. "Would she know about your multiple successes? Your vast experience? Your intimate knowledge of the business and the market?" "No," she responded. "She's been there for four years, and she hardly knows me."

If you don't tell them, how will they know?

The truth about creating a personal brand is you have to make it happen. Like all things, if you leave it to chance, the chance of it being exactly what you want it to be is virtually nil.

What do you think would have happened to Nike's sales if they'd just made some trainers and sports gear and shoved it on the shelves in some shops? That's essentially what you're doing by getting up each day and working your hardest, without also letting people know what you're up to. If you want to get known for being passionate and skilled at something, just doing the job isn't enough.

To create a leadership brand worth having, you first need to ask yourself some questions.

- What five words do you want people to use to describe you?
- What do you want to 'create' as a leader?
- What are you passionate about and what change do you want to create?
- What are your true talents and how do they add value to others?
- What are you an expert in or becoming expert in?
- What stories would you like others to tell about you?
- Who would you like to be associated with?
- What groups would you like to become active in – in and outside work?

Once you have an idea of the brand you're looking to create, think about who you'd like to know about you, and how you can get them to hear about you. Clearly, it's great for others to have read about you in articles, heard you on panels or watched you in a TED Talk, but the quickest, easiest and most accurate way for you to get the word out about who you really are… is for you to *tell them*.

Nailing your personal pitch

Imagine you're in a lift, and the senior leader of the division you want to work for, or the producer of a label you'd love to record your songs, walks in. She says hello and asks you if you are having a good day. This is your moment. You have 30 to 60 seconds to make your mark. Would you know what to say? Would you be totally prepared for this moment?

If the answer is no, then you need to be.

Extraordinary lives don't happen by chance. We need to make them happen. We need to take ownership; we need to be Rhinos; we need to take the shot. And if we're going to take the shot, we need to practise. As Michael Jordan famously said, "I've missed more than 9,000 shots in my career. I've lost almost 300 games. Twenty-six times, I've been trusted to take the game-winning shot and missed. I've failed over and over and over again in my life. And that is why I succeed."

Your personal pitch is your own game-winning shot.

It's what you say when someone asks you about yourself, and you have a few seconds to make a first impression. It's what you want to linger in their heads when they walk away so that, when they find themselves talking to someone who may be able to help you in a few weeks' time, they remember you and take action on your behalf.

When you think about how busy we all are, and how many thought-drones we have buzzing around in our head, that's no mean feat.

If I asked you to recite Nike's strapline out loud now, would you be able to? I'm guessing so. That's because they keep repeating *Just do it*: on posters, in TV ads, on their clothes, in social media. It's simple, it's clear, and it gets the message across. And that's what your pitch needs to be – clear, punchy and memorable. Plan it carefully.

On all of our programmes, we give people the opportunity to nail their pitch, and I cannot tell you the difference it makes to their careers within just a few months. When you're able to clearly articulate what it is about you that makes you stand out, what matters to you most, what you're focused on right now and what support you need to make it happen, you plug *your* extraordinary into the world – and you get extraordinary right back.

Bella had learnt about pitching while doing the Ivy House Award in school. It had become really clear in her mind that she wanted to study medicine, and that her main focus right now should be to get work experience.

While at her Saturday job in a local shop, a customer came in to return some items. Bella immediately thought she should call her manager as she wasn't sure how to do returns on the till. But, realising this was an opportunity to take ownership and learn, she decided to be courageous and have a go. What was the worst that could happen?

As she worked her way through the process, she chatted to the customer, telling her about her aspirations to go into medicine, why it was so important to her, and how she was trying to find some work experience. As it turned out, the customer was head of department at a big hospital. She gave Bella her contact details, and told her she was happy to explain all the ways she might be able to get the work experience she so desperately wanted.

If you don't ask, how will you get?

Most of us brought up in the UK (especially women, I'm sad to say), have had extreme modesty and self-deprecation drilled into us. We're taught to be self-effacing and understated, to leave others to blow our trumpet. But being brilliant and keeping it to yourself doesn't work. Your dream to do a certain job or meet a certain person has far more chance of working if you tell others about it – and no, it won't sound arrogant or pushy if you've practised doing it in the right way. Working on your pitch so you're ready to hit the ground running whenever the occasion arises will increase your chances of getting what you want a thousandfold.

So go back to those questions above, then pull together and practise your 'elevator pitch'. Remember, you want to cover four key elements:

What makes you worth remembering?

What are you focused on right now?

Why is it important to you?

And your question: what could you ask of them?

For a 30–60-second pitch, you'll need just a few sentences on each question. You might want to start by writing it down, though our experience shows that creating a mind map is more effective. Rather than tying yourself down to fixed sentences, a mind map gives you the freedom and flexibility to speak from the heart.

Once you've outlined your pitch, raise the stakes by imagining that the person you're pitching to is *exactly* who you need to kick-start your career/passion/project or the next phase in your extraordinary life. You could even print off a picture of them, if you know who they are.

Now keep practising – out loud – until you no longer need to refer to your mind map. Keep refining as you go. Is it as compelling as possible? Does it feel like an accurate reflection of you? Would you remember you? Ask people you trust to give you feedback. Then once you have something you're happy with, take one minute before you leave the house each day to quickly run through your pitch.

Feel weird? I don't care. Nor should you. If you only ever do things you're comfortable with, you're never going to get to a bigger, braver, more meaningful life, however hard you work. And the wonderful thing, the magical thing, is that when you ask others to help you reach your dreams, it's amazing what they'll do for you. Trust me. I've seen it time and time again. An awful lot of people out there want to help you reach your extraordinary.

They just don't know it yet.

RECAP
Human Leadership

- Human Leadership is the practice of leading oneself and others in a way that empowers everyone to reach their full potential. No matter who, what, or where you choose to lead, it's about creating environments of meaning, growth, belonging and ownership; enabling people, organisations and societies to thrive.

- It's also about making a living. All the evidence shows that Human Leadership is the most profitable form of leadership – creating teams that play to their strengths and doing work they love, is the most effective way to create successful organisations.

- Leadership can be broken down into the 'what' and 'how' of leadership. The 'what' is always the same, irrespective of the situation. Leaders must ensure there is a clear vision, a workable plan and the right environment to make it happen.

- The 'how' is always unique. It's dependent on the individual – who they are at their core, their knowledge, skills and ultimately the behaviour they choose.

- The world is changing and is affecting how we work and the kinds of jobs available. Leaders will not only need a different set of skills from those traditionally taught – they'll also need to take the development of those skills seriously.

- Human Leaders develop role-specific knowledge and skills, as well as fully developing each Extraordinary Skill. To do this they must:

  1. Take the time to understand their Core Strength, how to live from that place and enable others to do the same.

  2. Take 100% Ownership for where they are on the Ownership Ladder and the behaviour they choose in response to each event, expecting their team to do the same.

  3. Take responsibility for how they use their most powerful tool – their mind – and endeavour to operate from their Conscious Mind.

  4. Become Courageous Learners, being mindful of operating from above the line, being open to learning and change.

5. Create Intentional Relationships with individuals and teams – developing the art of effective conversations.

6. Practise Proactive Wellbeing – taking care to show up in their best state for their role as leader.

- Ultimately, we all have a choice about the kind of leader we become, the impact we have on individuals, organisations and societies. Human Leaders take this choice seriously – taking time to understand themselves, develop themselves and lead themselves. In this way they are able to create purpose-driven, values-led organisations.

The Reasons Why Not

There are so many reasons not to aim for an extraordinary life.

You're tired.

You're scared.

Things aren't so bad after all.

You enjoyed reading the book, and you agree with the whole 'stuff needs to change' vibe, but you've got a to-do list as long as your arm, and lunch needs making, and your friend wants to go out tonight, and that Netflix series is so good, and in short you're just too busy right now to commit to all that thinking and doing. You'll get to it later. Really, you will.

Except we never do, do we? And then we wake up ten, twenty, thirty years later and realise that we never did achieve everything we hoped for, never made enough time for our family, never spent our time in a way that felt meaningful and never had enough fun. And the world you live in is even more screwed up than it ever was.

We continue to believe that life is a struggle and, if we can just get to the end of the day, the week, the month, then we'll figure it out. But months pile on top of months, we get distracted, we get even busier and our moment to shift into a new way of being passes us by.

So this is your moment. This is your chance. This is your choice.

Are you in?

Are you in for going back and answering the questions, with honesty and curiosity and excitement?

Are you in for getting above the line, being courageous, climbing the Ownership Ladder, embracing Conscious Mind, and failing fast and forward every day?

Are you ready to connect with your inner wisdom, your deep knowing that will transform your life, right now?

If that's you, I'm glad we found each other.

Let's get started.

References

1   Mental Health Foundation, 'Statistics' <www.mentalhealth.org.uk/statistics>

2   Campaign to End Loneliness, 'Loneliness Research' <www.campaigntoendloneliness.org/loneliness-research>

3   Iulia-Cristina Uță, 'The Self-improvement Industry Is Estimated to Grow to $13.2 Billion by 2022' (Brand Minds, 27 June 2019) <https://brandminds.ro/the-self-improvement-industry-is-estimated-to-grow-to-13-2-billion-by-2022>

4   Julie Hani Fit4D, 'The Neuroscience of Behaviour Change' (Medium, 8 August 2017) <https://healthtransformer.co/the-neuroscience-of-behavior-change-bcb567fa83c1>

5   Kelly Bilodeau, 'Will a Purpose-driven Life Help You Live longer?' (Harvard Health Publishing, 28 November 2019) <www.health.harvard.edu/blog/will-a-purpose-driven-life-help-you-live-longer-2019112818378>

6   OECD Better Life Index, 'Life Satisfaction' <www.oecdbetterlifeindex.org/topics/life-satisfaction>

7   I first came across the Rhino idea in Scott Alexander, *Rhinoceros Success: The secret to charging full speed toward every opportunity* (Ramsey Press, 2003)

8   The Ownership Ladder appears in many different forms in the self and leadership development worlds – it's sometimes called the Accountability Ladder. The original creator is unknown.

9   Neringa Antanaityte, 'Mind Matters: How to effortlessly have more positive thoughts' (TLEX Institute) <https://tlexinstitute.com/how-to-effortlessly-have-more-positive-thoughts>

10   Carol S. Dweck, Ellen L. Leggett, 'A Social-cognitive Approach to Motivation and Personality' (1988) *Psychological Review*, Vol. 95, No. 2, 256–273

11   Matthew Syed, *Black Box Thinking: The surprising truth about success* (John Murray, 2015)

12   Liz Mineo, 'Good Genes Are Nice, but Joy is Better' (*The Harvard Gazette*, 11 April 2017) <https://news.harvard.edu/gazette/story/2017/04/over-nearly-80-years-harvard-study-has-been-showing-how-to-live-a-healthy-and-happy-life>

13   Joe Smith, 'Loneliness on its way to become Britain's most lethal condition' (Independent, 30 April 2018) <https://www.independent.co.uk/life-style/health-and-families/loneliness-lethal-condition-therapy-psychology-cox-commission-ons-health-a8311781.html>

14   Stephen B. Karpman, 'Fairy tales and script drama analysis' (1968) *Transactional Analysis Bulletin*, 7(26), 39–43 <www.karpmandramatriangle.com/pdf/DramaTriangle.pdf>

15   Jenny Odell, *How to Do Nothing: Resisting the attention economy* (Melville House Publishing, 2019)

16   Jenny Odell, 'How to Do Nothing' (Medium, 30 June 2017) <https://medium.com/@the_jennitaur/how-to-do-nothing-57e100f59bbb>

17   Jim Dethmer, Diana Chapman and Kaley Warner Klemp, *The 15 Commitments of Conscious Leadership: A new paradigm for sustainable success* (Dethmer Chapman & Klemp, 2015)

18 William Duggan's research in *Strategic Intuition: The Creative spark in human achievement*, as quoted in *The 15 Commitments of Conscious Leadership*, Jim Dethmer, Diana Chapman and Kaley Warner Klemp (2014), p212

19 Clara M. Davis, 'Results of the Self-selection of Diets by Young Children' (1939) Seventieth Annual Meeting, Canadian Medical Association, Section of Paediatrics, Montreal <www.ncbi.nlm.nih.gov/pmc/articles/PMC537465/pdf/canmedaj00208-0035.pdf>

20 University of Colorado at Boulder, 'Your Brain on Imagination: It's a lot like reality, study shows' (ScienceDaily, 10 December 2018) <www.sciencedaily.com/releases/2018/12/181210144943.htm>

21 Jim Harter, 'Why Some Leaders Have Their Employees' Trust, and Some Don't' (Gallup, 13 June 2019) <www.gallup.com/workplace/258197/why-leaders-employees-trust-don.aspx>

22 Mental Health Foundation, 'Mental Health Statistics: Stress' (2018) <www.mentalhealth.org.uk/statistics/mental-health-statistics-stress>

23 Nathan Martin, 'Three Ways Employers Can Prepare for the Future of Work' (Virgin, 16 August 2019) <www.virgin.com/virgin-unite/three-ways-employers-can-prepare-future-work>

24 Forbes, *Fostering Innovation Through a Diverse Workforce* <https://images.forbes.com/forbesinsights/StudyPDFs/Innovation_Through_Diversity.pdf>

25 Rocío Lorenzo, Nicole Voigt, Miki Tsusaka, Matt Krentz and Katie Abouzahr, 'How Diverse Leadership Teams Boost Innovation' (BCG, 23 January 2018) <www.bcg.com/en-us/publications/2018/how-diverse-leadership-teams-boost-innovation.aspx>

26 Karl Thompson, 'What Percentage of Your Life Will You Spend at Work?' (ReviseSociology, 16 August 2016) <https://revisesociology.com/2016/08/16/percentage-life-work>

27 Susie Cranston and Scott Keller, 'Increasing the "Meaning Quotient' of Work' (McKinsey Quarterly, 1 January 2013) <www.mckinsey.com/business-functions/organization/our-insights/increasing-the-meaning-quotient-of-work>

28   Korn Ferry, 'A Better Return on Self-awareness' <www.kornferry.com/insights/articles/better-return-self-awareness>

29   IDA, 'Jobskifte og Motivation for Mobilitet' (2016) <https://ida.dk/media/2426/jobskifte_og_motivation_for_mobilitet_endelig_.pdf?>

30   Amy Cuddy, *Presence: Bringing Your Boldest Self to Your Biggest Challenges* (Little, Brown Spark, 2015)

31   Jessica Tyler, 'The Value of Conversations With Employees' (Gallup Business Journal, 30 June 2011) <https://news.gallup.com/businessjournal/147749/value-conversations-employees.aspx>

32   Z_punkt, University of South Wales, and UK Commission for Employment and Skills, *The Future of Work: Jobs and Skills in 2030* <https://dera.ioe.ac.uk//19601>

33   Morten Albæk, *One Life: How we forgot to live meaningful lives* (LID Publishing, 2018) pp28–29

34   André Martin and Vidula Bal, *The State of Teams* (Center for Creative Leadership) <www.ccl.org/wp-content/uploads/2015/04/StateOfTeams.pdf>

35   Alex Therrien, 'Fifth of 14-year-old Girls in UK "Have Self-harmed"' (BBC, 29 August 2018) <www.bbc.co.uk/news/health-45329030>

36   Scott Aronin and Matthew Smith, 'One in Four Students Suffer from Mental Health Problems' (YouGov, 9 August 2016) <https://yougov.co.uk/topics/lifestyle/articles-reports/2016/08/09/quarter-britains-students-are-afflicted-mental-hea>

37   Josh Wilson, 'Work-related stress and mental illness now accounts for over half of work absences' (*The Telegraph*, 1 November 2018) <www.telegraph.co.uk/news/2018/11/01/work-related-stress-mental-illness-now-accounts-half-work-absences>

Recommended further reading

On Purpose
What Are You Really Here to Do?
Steve Chamberlain

One Life
How We Forgot to Live Meaningful Lives
Morten Albæk

Somebody Should Have Told Us!
Simple Truths for Living Well
Jack Pransky

The 15 Commitments of Conscious Leadership
A New Paradigm for Sustainable Success
Jim Dethmer, Diana Chapman and Kaley Warner Klemp

The Element
How Finding Your Passion Changes Everything
Ken Robinson

The Inside Out Revolution
The Only Thing You Need to Know to Change Your Life Forever
Michael Neill

The Monk Who Sold His Ferrari
Robin Sharma

The Space Within
Finding Your Way Back Home
Michael Neill

The Untethered Soul
The Journey Beyond Yourself
Michael A. Singer

Acknowledgements

This book is dedicated to the people without whom this book would never have been written: our five daughters, Emmi, Lara, Meg, Sian, Mimi, and the delegates of every single Ivy House programme so far, who together have taught me more than any book or course ever could, as well as fuelled my passion to change how we develop each generation going forward.

This book is a rallying call. It's a call for you to step up and become the leaders of your lives as well as the leaders we so desperately need. Thank you for letting me in. Thank you for helping me learn. Thank you for trusting me. Working with you all has been the greatest privilege of my life so far. Your energy, openness to learning, your ability to challenge the status quo and determination to create lives worth living, leaves me excited for the future. Stay connected to your strength. Stay connected to us.

Talking of which, I want to thank the phenomenal Ivy House team. Working with people determined to bring these game-changing leadership and life skills to every generation is a complete privilege. Clare Mitchell, Andy Kelsey, Lindsay Terris, Bryony Don, Caroline Heanley, Laura Jelly, Deandra Murphy, Vicky Gerrish, Kate Lander, Steve Chamberlain, Dani Brooks, Darren Smallridge, Ray Martin, Amanda Wilby, Tim Hewitt, Helena Clayton – your expertise, commitment, humility, debate, friendship and totally dodgy humour make coming to work a joy, even when the going gets tough. Kate particularly – thank you for steering the Ivy House ship so brilliantly and giving me the space to be in my element.

In working on this book I'm indebted to the brilliant Molly Flatt, whose almost magical talent with words and editorial prowess has helped make it far better than it would have been. Molly, you are a wonder. And Clare Mitchell, who has debated every phrase, looked at a thousand badly drawn diagrams and challenged me to be better. Clare, thank you. You are a hero. Patrick Fogarty and Laura Jelly, who are two of the most creative people I know and have worked together passionately to make this book reflect the energy of Ivy House. Stephen Wood – such a creative and deep thinker as well as dispenser of invaluable feedback. Steve Chamberlain, who, as always, has been a great support through this process.

Also, huge love and gratitude to my family and amazing friends, who, as I have trodden this path, often absent for weeks on end, have supported, loved and encouraged me in every way. Marc, you are more than anyone could wish for in a brother, always there for me, both professionally and personally – I am ever thankful someone decided we were to take this journey together. Mum and Dad, you showed me what real courage looks like – not accepting the path laid out for you but creating your own, and Justin, for giving me the confidence *not* to think myself too small. To Claire, Suse and Katherine, for your deep friendship, your belief in me and your hands-on and invaluable support with reading and proofing the book. But most importantly, for your ability to find the best bottle of rosé and the best seat in the sun, and to laugh at whatever life brings. I am one of those lucky people who have found their purpose as well as the relationships that bring joy to my life.

And finally, Chris, my gorgeous husband. Quite simply, you rock. You gave me the time, space, love and support to become me. Your unswerving belief in what is possible and my ability to achieve it has been life-changing – I will love you forever.

About Ivy House

At Ivy House we're on a mission to put game-changing leadership and life skills at the heart of how we develop every generation. We turn leadership development on its head, broadening the concept of leadership, teaching different skills and doing it far earlier – at a time in a person's life when it can make the biggest difference.

We deliver the kind of transformational personal and professional development that has previously only been available to a tiny percentage of senior executives, to talent throughout organisations and schools, giving them the knowledge and skills to become extraordinary leaders and lead extraordinary lives.

Whether you're part of a forward-looking organisation wanting to future-proof your talent development strategy, or a school passionate about preparing your students to succeed in a very different world – our programmes don't just nurture your brightest people; they will transform your results and build leaders who have the ability to change the world. The kind of leaders people actually want to follow and pioneers who are equipped to lead us all into a better future.

To find out more about how we can support the talent within your organisation or your sixth formers, get in touch today.

in Ivy House London
Ivy House World
Ivy House Lon
Ivy House London

Wait, there's more...

To continue on your Courageous Learner journey, subscribe to the 'Extraordinary Unplugged' podcast.

In this series, I talk with Ivy House alumni and others on their journeys to create their extraordinary lives. In these conversations we unpick some of the challenges that have held them back from living their extraordinary lives – and give you practical support and advice so that you can live yours.

You can find 'Extraordinary Unplugged' online at
https://anchor.fm/ivyhouse.

Listen on your favourite podcast platform, subscribe and share!

Printed in Great Britain
by Amazon

26626893R00155